The Tangled Web

~ Chronicles of Deception ~

Robin Stone

~ A compelling true-life experience ~

The Tangled Web

Tellwell Talent
www.tellwell.ca

ISBN
978-0-2288-3062-7 (Hardcover)
978-0-2288-3061-0 (Paperback)
978-0-2288-3063-4 (eBook)

This book is dedicated to the memory of my sister who is sadly missed every day, my estranged brother who is loved more than he will ever know, and my husband who supported and encouraged me every step of the way; I will hold you in my heart forever.

"The sorrow we feel when we lose
a loved one is the price we pay for
having had them in our lives"
~ Rob Liano

I would like to send out a word of thanks to all my friends who helped to put a shine on my writing; Eraina, Brenda, Wendy, Christina, Audrey and Joanne, thank you!

In addition, kudos to Rebecca, my editor at Tellwell Publishers, who, when I was faltering and left wondering if my story held any merit gave a wonderfully encouraging review of my writing, thank you!

“Sometimes, a story is a letter the author writes to himself, to tell himself things that he would not to be able to understand otherwise”

~ Carlos Ruiz Zafon

This book was written for the sole purpose of bringing attention to what I feel is a serious problem facing the public today. My story is factual therefore, the names and locations have been altered to protect the individuals, associations, and institutions mentioned within these pages.

Preface

The dictionary describes a Predator as someone who ruthlessly exploits others. Distinctively characterized by their lack of emotion they show no pity or compassion for their victims. Masters of manipulation and lacking in empathy they set out to capture their prey. Zeroing in on the weak and vulnerable they go in for the kill. Exploiting their victims by taking advantage of them unethically and unjustly for their own benefit, they leave behind a trail of shattered lives.

My initial intent for writing this timeline of events was to gather all the facts, along with my personal knowledge to gain a better understanding of the gravity of the unbearable circumstances my family was forced to endure, over the course of our harrowing involvement with a Predator.

The devastation inflicted upon my family by this woman is irreversible. Akin to Post Traumatic Stress Disorder, we have all been left licking our wounds, shaking our heads, and wondering *what the hell just happened?* Looking back and realizing the skill this woman possessed in producing the constant confusion and chaos, surrounding each and every encounter we had with her, is to say at the least unsettling.

Her defiance of the obvious truth bordered on delusion as she kept to her shameless lies at all cost. When her self-gratifying twisted view of reality created doubt and was questioned, she put it down to coincidence, leaving no room for argument. As an opportunist, she was able to pick up on any situation appearing to have the slightest chance of enhancing her own personal finances or bolstering her ego.

The driving force compelling me to go forward with this book was an attempt to bring attention to the injustices and possibly gain a plausible explanation for how and why such blatant acts of defiance were allowed to go unaccounted for. In my search for the answer it became clear; I was the only person with complete knowledge of every aspect of this insidious situation. There is no one else who knows the entire truth other than the Predator herself.

With so many fragmented and disjointed components to this story it would have been impossible to piece the events together unless you had been involved in every step of this perplexing experience from the very beginning. As such, I feel it is not only my right but my integral duty to put forward the knowledge and understanding I possess of this tangled web of deceit, as I observed it unfold.

They say everyone has a story to tell, this is mine.....

~ Chapter One ~

*"The best and most beautiful things
in this world cannot be seen or even heard
but must be felt with the heart."
~ Helen Keller*

The lure of a simpler, less complicated way of life resulted in Doug and I relocating to the little farming town of Fairport in southeastern Ontario in the spring of 2001. After discovering a lovely fixer upper nestled on the banks of the Sydenbrae, we knew immediately this is where we wanted to spend the rest of our lives. With excitement and enthusiasm we began creating a wonderful world for ourselves. Almost a decade has passed since then and we are just as intrigued by the charm of living here as the day we arrived. Small town living has exceeded our expectations and offered us everything we hoped it would. The informal pace of the small, rural town we chose to call home allowed us to create a comforting and satisfying lifestyle for ourselves. Cradled in the arms of contentment, we felt nothing could disrupt our peace of mind as we settled into enjoying the sweet rewards of our senior years and life was good!

On October 31, 2011, after handing out the last of the treats, Doug offered to blow out the candle in the pumpkin and turn the porch light off while I put the kettle on for tea. As we sat enjoying our evening tradition of mulling over the events of the day, we talked about how great it was for the kids to be able to make their rounds without the usual downpour we'd come to expect on Halloween. Then, chuckling to ourselves we recalled how inventive their costumes were and remarked on how much they'd all grown over the past year. After savoring the last sip we decided it was time to call it a day. Before reaching the bedroom I stopped to give Sarah, my younger sister, one more call. I'd left a message earlier on her answering machine. I was anxious to speak to her directly to congratulate her on a job well done. I was hoping she would pick up.

You see, that day a program called "Puppy Luv" aired on TV. The gist of the show was that every week, three different breeds of puppies, along with their breeders were featured. A family was selected to visit all three breeders and after spending time with the puppies, they were asked to pick which breed of puppy fit their lifestyle best. At the end of the program, the family would take their chosen puppy home with them. That night Sarah just happened to be one of the three breeders highlighted on the show.

Specializing in breeding world class Maltese puppies, Sarah was thrilled at being asked to take part in the show. Maltese, as they are commonly known are a miniature breed, originating from Malta. They are famous for producing the most adorable, fluffy balls of fur, resembling miniature sheepdogs when they mature, making them simply irresistible! Earlier that evening, Doug and I remained on the edge of our seats, as we watched the show and we were delighted when we saw the family pick Sarah's puppy to take home with them. Somehow, she'd managed to keep the results a secret and I couldn't wait to tell her how proud I was of her sudden claim to fame.

I was so excited for her when I thought of how all the publicity surrounding the show would help to promote the breed and the kennel she so aptly called, "Puppy Haven". She had worked long and hard to produce her signature Maltese puppies. They were her life and she prided herself in pampering them from the day they were born, until the moment they left to go to their forever homes. What a relief it was to see her finally receiving recognition for all her time and effort.

I dialed her number and when the answering machine came on I left another message. Finding it hard to control my excitement about the results of the show I gushed with pride into the machine, congratulating her and asking her to give me a call in the morning. By now, it was past eleven and I figured she'd gone to help our younger brother Mark get made up for Halloween and most likely ended up staying to watch the show with him. Sarah said they'd been planning his costume for days and told me how excited he was about going out trick or treating. She wanted his costume to be a surprise for me, so she said she'd email me a picture of him when he was all dressed up and ready to go out the door. I took a moment to wonder what he had chosen to be this year, Batman, a Vampire or maybe Elvis. Those were his all-time favorites and I could only imagine how worked up he would be by the time he was ready to leave the house.

By the way, Mark just so happens to be my amazing brother, who has special needs. He is a fifty seven year old man who embraces life with the mind of a child. Being the epitome of innocence, he still enjoys dressing up and going door to door for Halloween, still believes in the wonders of Santa and still waits for the Easter Bunny to hide his chocolate eggs on Easter morning. He would have been thrilled to see Sarah and her puppies on TV, especially when it was Sarah's puppy that was picked over the others.

Once I settled into bed it didn't take long to drift off. Sometime later, I was suddenly jarred out of my dream state by a loud knocking at the door. Struggling to fully wake up I heard Doug grumbling as he made his way to see who it was.

"Who on earth could that be at this time of night? I sure hope it's not those older kids still out there looking for treats!" He mumbled under his breath.

Glancing at the clock I could see it was a little after one o'clock in the morning. Doubtful that it would be trick or treaters at that time of night I strained to hear what was being said but I couldn't quite make anything out. A few minutes later Doug came into the bedroom. One look at his face and I knew something was horribly wrong.

He came and sat next to me on the edge of the bed.

"What? What is it?" I questioned impatiently.

Immediately I felt my heart begin to pound in my chest and my mind began to race as I anticipated the endless possibilities of what his answer could be. After what seemed to be an eternity he whispered,

"It's Sarah."

"What about Sarah?" I urged.

Again, after what seemed like an endless pause, he took my hand and replied, "There's been a terrible accident."

"Oh God! No! Not Sarah!" I cried out, as what he was implying began to sink in.

"The police are here. They'd like to speak to you." He whispered.

My body numbed as my mind scattered to make sense of the dreadful reality unfolding before me. With the help of Doug, I managed to make my way to the living room where a policeman stood waiting.

Reading the look on my face the officer could see I'd already been told the devastating news. He removed his cap and began to explain,

"There was a single car accident not far from Hampton, on County Road 21, around nine o'clock this evening".

Then, as if listening through a dense fog of emotion, I heard him say,

"Your sister's vehicle left the road at 130 kilometers an hour, rolled a number of times and ended up in a farmer's field. She was killed instantly."

He then offered his condolences and apologized for the delay in contacting me, but apparently they had a difficult time tracking me down.

Unable to grasp the reality of what I was being told, I asked in desperation,

"Are you sure it was my sister? Maybe they've made a mistake. Maybe it wasn't Sarah after all."

He looked straight at me and stated apologetically, "No Ma'am, there's been no mistake. I'm sorry."

Shaken to the very core of my being I collapsed into the chair and began to weep uncontrollably. Desperately, my mind searched to find a comfortable place where I could comprehend what I'd just been told. I was finally forced to accept there was simply no way to make sense of the devastating news. I was suspended in disbelief. It was beyond my realm of understanding to think my sister was dead.

How is that even possible? I just spoke to her yesterday. I whispered to myself as Doug and the officer continued their conversation.

Fully engaged with my innermost thoughts, I vaguely remember the officer asking if I would be OK. Somehow, I managed to give him a feeble nod as reassurance of my acceptance of the unimaginable news I'd just been told. Then he turned and Doug led him to the front door.

Once Doug and I were alone, we went into the kitchen where we sat motionless, absorbed in our own secluded worlds. I have no idea of how much time went by before Doug finally broke into the silence,

"I know it's late, but we'd better call Carla to let her know what's happened. Mark will have to be told."

Carla is Mark's hired caregiver and when I spoke to Sarah the day before she said Mark would be staying with Carla and her partner Matt over the next few days. I stood braced against the wall while Doug dialed the number. When Carla answered I recall him repeating the tragic news and asking if he could speak to Mark. Apparently, Mark was in bed so Doug asked Carla to have him call us as soon as he woke up. They spoke for quite a while after that and when he hung up the phone he relayed their conversation to me.

"Carla says she knew what happened to Sarah right after the accident occurred but didn't call us because she didn't want to wake us up. Mark already knows about everything and from what Carla says, he's taking it pretty hard."

"That's odd." I noted out loud. "She could have called us. The accident took place around nine and it's not likely we'd be sleeping at that time of night."

Doug continued, "Apparently, Sarah showed up there around noon yesterday, after she'd been to the lawyers to sign the final papers for the house. She spent the afternoon getting Mark made up for Halloween and then stayed to watch the show with him. After the show, Carla's partner Matt left with her and Mark to go shelling out and because they recorded the show earlier Sarah decided to stay behind to watch it again. By the time they arrived back home Sarah was gone. They tried calling her house and when they didn't get an answer, Matt and Carla's daughter, Jennifer, went out looking for her. They traced her usual route home but when they got to the junction of Highway 40 and County Road 21, the police had the road barricaded off because there had been an accident. Matt and Jennifer tried to get information about who was involved in the accident and what condition they were in. The officer they spoke to said it was a woman who was killed instantly after running off the road but was unable to give them any further information. Jennifer said she was able to look over the officer's shoulder and make out Sarah's name on his clipboard and with that they left. Carla says she had them take Sarah to the funeral home in town, so, I told her we'd meet them there first thing in the morning."

After Doug finished, something just wasn't making sense to me, so, I asked,

"If she already knew about the accident and had Sarah sent to the funeral home she must have been speaking with the police. Why didn't she tell them how to contact us? After all, it's not like we're strangers, she knows our number and she knows exactly where we live."

Doug just shrugged his shoulders and said, "I don't know why Carla doesn't do a lot of things. I really don't."

Feeling as if I was living out a nightmare, I somehow managed to find the strength to call my three girls to tell them the unthinkable news about their Auntie Sarah. They too were in shock and disbelief when I passed on the few details I knew to share with them at the time. After telling them we were leaving in the morning to meet Carla at the funeral home I hung up, promising to call as soon as we arrived back home.

The remainder of the night was heart wrenching. Tossing and turning I was fixated on recreating my sister's accident over and over in my mind. Through a steady stream of tears I tried desperately to visualize what her final moments would have been like. Asking myself the same questions repeatedly, *What was she thinking at the time? What was she feeling? Did she suffer?* Agonizing over the tragedy of it all made sleep impossible. Periodically, Doug would try to comfort me but I simply wasn't open to being comforted that night. My visualizations were vivid, my pain was sharp and my thoughts were unceasing.

By morning, exhausted and consumed with the full impact of my grief, tears continued to flow as we set out on a four hour journey to where my sister's body lay. During the seemingly endless drive there was very little said between Doug and me. By this point our tattered emotions had fully embraced us and it was as if words just got in the way of feeling.

Once we arrived at our destination and upon entering the funeral home I was snapped into a world where everything felt foreign and surreal. From that moment on I merely went through the motions. We were a little early, so, we decided to wait inside for

Matt and Carla to arrive. A short time later we were surprised to see them coming down from upstairs with Mark at their side. They were accompanied by the funeral director who escorted us into a private sitting room. Once we were all seated comfortably he turned to Doug and me and began to explain.

"Carla, as executor of Sarah's will, has just finished making the final arrangements with me and she has decided Sarah will be cremated. This will be carried out on Thursday. If you wish to spend time with your sister, to say your final goodbyes, you may make arrangements for a viewing through Carla."

Choosing to cherish my final memories of Sarah I declined his offer. Without hesitation, I told him I would prefer to remember my sister exactly the way I saw her last. In my mind's eye I pictured her smiling and waving goodbye to us as we drove away from her place earlier that month.

Even though I was aware of Sarah appointing Carla to be executor of her will, I wasn't prepared emotionally for the underlying implications. After having the chance to mull over what the director had just said to me I became furious to think I would have to make arrangements with Carla, a paid caregiver, to say my final goodbyes to my sister. Sitting there I felt like a complete stranger as it was made perfectly clear to me Carla was the executor of Sarah's will and in total charge of all and any final arrangements. Clearly, I had no say in anything from this point on. Fighting back tears and the urge to run out of there I anguished over the position I'd found myself in. Very quickly I came to realize the executor's opinions and decisions reigned supreme, leaving me to tend to my wounded heart in silence. The director then pointed out to me,

"A decision on the venue and the final funeral arrangements hasn't been settled as yet but Carla has already written up the obituary and we will be sending it in to the paper today."

This was news to me and I was stunned to think something this important was going to be sent out without me at least seeing it first, so I asked if I could read it. After going over the write up I realized there was barely a mention of Sarah's family at all while Carla managed to successfully highlight herself. Knowing Carla the way I did, I wasn't surprised to see the oversight of her adding Mark and I as an afterthought. The disrespect Carla harboured towards my family was unmistakable and according to her past behavior was almost expected, even so, it was upsetting but not worth causing a scene over. I simply asked the director if I could have a little time to add a few names and comments on behalf of the family. He paused, turned to Carla for her approval and when she agreed he told me I had until the following morning to hand the changes in to him or it would be printed as is. As a result, plans were made for Doug and me to meet there first thing the next day with the revised obituary.

After leaving the funeral home that day, we gathered outside with Matt and Carla to talk things over but as I glanced over at Mark, standing off to the side, it was obvious he was hurting. The pain, so plainly etched into his face, touched me deeply resulting in me being persuaded to come out of my own self-absorbed anguish long enough to realize I wasn't the only one suffering. Going over to him to share in his pain I felt an overwhelming closeness to him. Then with tear filled eyes, we embraced and he sadly shared his feelings with me,

"Tera not here no more, Wobin! She gone to be with Mom and Dad in heben!"

Taking his hands in mine, my heart went out to him while I tried to ease his pain.

"I know Mark. It's OK. Everything will be fine. I'll make sure of that. You'll see."

There was no way of knowing exactly what Mark's perception of this situation was but I could see whatever it was, he was feeling it very intensely. Sensing his profound naivety and innocence towards the loss of our sister, I was overcome with a great sense of duty to protect him.

Carla came over to us and abruptly disrupted our private moment to say a friend of hers and Sarah's, who lived in town, had offered to hold the memorial in her home and she just wanted to know what I thought of the idea. After thinking it over for a moment, I told her I thought it was a wonderful suggestion. A private memorial held in a friend's home seemed more fitting for Sarah than holding a formal service for her in a funeral home.

After agreeing on the venue for the memorial, Carla suggested, while we were in the area we should plan to stop by Sarah's house the following day, to pick up anything of hers we might want to take back with us. We really weren't prepared for this but Carla insisted it be done as soon as possible. She feared that once Robert found out about Sarah's accident, he'd lock the doors and not let anyone in to get anything. The mere fact Robert wasn't aware of Sarah's death by now came as a shock to me.

Let me explain. Robert had been Sarah's partner for eight years and even though their relationship ended bitterly over a year ago, Doug and I remained friends with him. Although what Carla was saying seemed to be out of character for him, at the time, we were too self-involved with our grief to fully comprehend the meaning of what she was claiming. We agreed to meet at Sarah's after we dropped the obituary off the following morning.

Doug and I had made arrangements to stay that night with friends who lived not far from where Sarah lived. It was always nice to be able to spend time with them when we were in the area but it was especially comforting to have someone to lean on in our time of mourning. Their consoling words were incredibly supportive and welcomed after the exhausting day we'd just been through. Assuming there was another hectic day in store for us the following day we decided to retire to bed early. Sleep didn't come easily that night as I tossed and turned till dawn. Wrestling with my thoughts and trying to come to terms with my disheveled feelings made me thankful when I saw the first rays of sunshine peek through the shades in the morning.

The moment my eyes were open, the reality of Carla's request to meet at Sarah's began to ambush my thoughts. It had only been two days since the accident and I felt it was disrespectful to Sarah's memory to enter her home and go through her things so soon after her passing. Carla's request to meet at Sarah's began to seem inconceivable to me. It just didn't seem appropriate no matter how I tried to justify it; but on the other hand, it was still Robert's house and if what she was saying was true I certainly didn't want to take the chance of losing any family keepsakes or precious photos Sarah possessed. Feeling pressured into going ahead with this invasion was against my better judgment but I felt I had no choice.

Matt, Carla and, Mark were already waiting for us at the funeral home when we arrived and after getting Carla's approval, the obituary was sent off to be printed. After this Carla and I decided to confirm our decision to hold a private memorial in a friend's house. We both agreed Sarah would have been pleased with our choice. Carla then advised the director of our plans and let him know we would not be using their facility for a service. Then, we all got into our vehicles after planning to meet at Sarah's place in an hour.

What I was about to do, so soon after Sarah's death, seemed unimaginable to me and I just couldn't believe I was about to go ahead with this plan. As we pulled into the driveway my heart sank. Everything felt so lifeless, so desolate. There were no lights on, there were no puppies running around the yard and most importantly Sarah wasn't at the front door smiling, with open arms welcoming us to come in. Instead, Carla was standing on the porch struggling to get the door open with Matt and Mark waiting patiently behind her. Once the door was finally pushed open and I stepped in, I paused to peek at the freshly decorated room Sarah had recently done over. I recalled how proud she was that she'd managed to breathe new life into this old house. This is where she planned to begin rebuilding her life. This was her dream, but sadly a dream that would never be fulfilled.

Once inside, I made my way across the room to the china cabinet where the dishes our mother handed down to Sarah were so proudly displayed. To me they were a very important part of our family tradition. They represented all the celebrations we enjoyed together over the years. As I began carefully wrapping and placing the china into boxes I happened to notice three partially assembled dressers in the living room and remembered the day Sarah told me she'd ordered them. On top of one of the dressers was a signed form for foster care from Children's Services. I recall how excited Sarah was about being accepted as a foster parent and how busy she'd been preparing the rooms, in time for the girls to arrive. I could almost hear her voice as I thought of our most recent conversations.

A sense of melancholy washed over me. Suddenly, I felt passionately disturbed as I realized the significance of where I was and what I was doing.

My head began to swim, my legs weakened and tears began to well up inside. I was completely overcome with grief and began sobbing uncontrollably. I honestly didn't know how I was going to get through this day but somehow, after releasing a storehouse of pent up emotions, I managed to regain my composure.

During this entire time Carla stood across the room, propped against the front door with her arms folded across her chest, staring at the floor as if she was waiting for me to finish with what I was doing so she could get on with her day. I was given the distinct impression she was being inconvenienced while I gathered the few things I'd come for.

Suddenly, she looked over at me and hollered out, "Take whatever you want. I won't fight you for it!"

I was taken back by her comment. *What a strange thing to say,* I considered as I felt my guard go up.

In the midst of my grief I was sensitive to the boldness of Carla's presence. The harsh impact of her words coupled with the bitterness I already harbored towards her began to well up within me, so when she announced she was going to the office to make a phone call, I felt relieved to be left alone to deal with my emotions in private.

A few minutes later, I heard her scream from the office,

"Get the hell out of here and never go into this room again!"

I spun around to see Mark sheepishly coming out of the office. Apparently he had walked in on a private phone call she was having. It was obvious she wasn't pleased about him coming into the room unannounced. Troubled by her explosive tone towards him I put it down to her just trying to cope with her own grief. So, after taking time to console Mark I chose to ignore the incident in order to stay focused on the task at hand.

After carefully packing the dishes, I made my way down the hall towards the bedroom to see where Sarah would have kept her jewelry. Before Mom passed away, she divided her collection of jewelry between me and Sarah and passed it on to us. Dad had always prided himself in giving our Mom expensive jewelry as gifts. Having a great eye for quality, over the years he purchased some beautiful pieces for her. In addition, Mom had inherited a number of fine pieces of jewelry from our grandmother. These were also divided and passed down to Sarah and me. I felt strongly about these treasures remaining in the family and I was hoping to bring Sarah's collection home with me.

As I entered the bedroom, I glanced around the room and could see there was no sign of a jewelry box. Suspecting she may have kept her valuables hidden in one of her drawers, I started opening them, one by one. At that moment I could feel Sarah's presence around me and I found myself chanting silently, *forgive me, Sarah! Please forgive me!* Tears streamed down my cheeks and lay on her neatly folded cloths, only to be absorbed and dissipate moments later. Silly, but at that moment I felt as if Sarah was right there trying to console me, wiping away my tears. When I finished searching all the dresser drawers and found nothing, I happened to notice Carla leaning against the bedroom door her eyes following my every move, making me feel very uneasy but I was on a mission so I continued with my search in spite of her.

Moving on to the bedside table I was relieved when I opened the top drawer and saw a number of jewelry cases inside. While sorting through the contents of the drawer and carefully placing the cases into a bag I felt Carla hovering over me. I suddenly felt like an intruder and wanted nothing better than to finish up what I was doing so I could get out of my sister's house, as soon as possible. There were just too many reminders, too many memories, too many feelings and then, of course, there was Carla. It was just too soon for me to be doing this to begin with but having Carla there watching my every move made it unbearable. Without realizing it I began frantically throwing everything into the bag. Finally, mission accomplished, I was able to leave the room with the jewelry in hand and Carla right on my heels.

As I passed by the office on my way to the living room, I caught sight of an arrangement of framed photos and diplomas hanging on the wall. I knew they held a special meaning for Sarah, so I took a moment to carefully wrap them and sadly placed them in a box. When I reached the living room Doug and Matt were just coming in from outside. Doug announced he had collected the fountain and the two boxes containing Mom and Dad's ashes from the garden. I stopped what I was doing and tearfully remembered how, shortly after Sarah moved into the house, she had buried their ashes in the side garden and beautifully displayed the little angel fountain in honor of their memory. Now I planned to bring them home with me.

One final look around the living room and I noticed a painting of Katie, one of Sarah's favorite prize winning puppies. I had painted this for her birthday, the year before. Remembering how she cried when I gave it to her and how much she loved it, I removed it from the wall and put it in the box along with the other pictures. Taking a moment to ponder the memories of that special day brought a sudden surge of tears to my eyes. Lastly, I noticed an old wooden chest belonging to our Grandfather who was a carpenter by trade and for many years used the trunk to carry his tools in. Sarah had repurposed it and used it as her coffee table. I asked the guys if they wouldn't mind carrying it out to the van. Satisfied I had collected everything that held meaning for the family, we literally stuffed everything into the back of the van. Then, as I turned and saw Carla closing the front door behind us, I once again became consumed with sadness knowing I would never enter through those doors again and have Sarah waiting on the other side to welcome us.

Before leaving for home we all gathered for a few moments on the porch to talk. Matt began the conversation by saying there was a great deal of drinking going on at Carla's on the day of the accident. That was no surprise to us, we expected as much but when Carla took over the conversation and said she stayed back with Sarah to watch the tape of the show while Matt, Jennifer and Mark went out trick or treating, both Doug and I caught the obvious contradiction in her story. Previously, on the night of the accident, while speaking to Doug on the phone Carla told him it was Matt, Carla and Mark who went out and Sarah stayed home alone to watch the show. Doug and I remained silent about her conflicted statement as she added how terrible she felt about not removing the keys from Sarah's truck that night, knowing she had too much to drink to be able to drive safely.

Then Matt cut into the conversation. "You know we were always following Sarah home when she'd been drinking at our place. A couple of times we found her passed out at the side of the road. In fact," he went on to say, "one time she flew off the road and rolled over a couple of times, landed upright on someone's lawn and remained passed out behind the wheel but luckily we were able to get her out of there and get her home before the cops came."

Laughing as if it were some kind of game they played with her, he continued to say,

"I just knew this was bound to happen sometime. I guess it was inevitable".

"Leave it up to Sarah to leave with a bang." Carla jested.

Shocked by their insensitive bantering, I asked myself, *did I hear them correctly? Bound to happen, inevitable, leave with a bang!?* I was left stunned by their tactless remarks and the lack of respect they had for my sister.

Just then a neighbor of Sarah's came walking up the driveway leaving me feeling glad for the diversion. It gave a welcome break from the troubling conversation we were having. Matt excused himself and went over to speak to the woman. He no sooner began speaking to her when Carla ran over and whisked her back down the driveway. A few minutes later Carla returned to where we were all gathered, saying the woman just wanted to give her condolences.

Then, turning to Matt she snapped, "Watch what you say to people!"

Wow! What an odd thing for her to say to him! I noted.

Carla, noticing my uneasiness changed the subject and went on to say, "Sarah went to the lawyers in the morning to sign what I thought were the final papers for possession of the house but what I didn't realize is Sarah still had to deliver them to Robert's lawyer for the final signature.

I wasn't prepared to listen to Carla convey her side of the story about the day of the accident, so I took the first chance I had to turn the conversation towards Mark by asking Carla if she would mind continuing to look after him until I had the time to give some serious thought about his care.

She answered saying, "Sure we'll keep him with us. That shouldn't be a problem at all."

I felt relieved to hear her answer because I knew I wouldn't be able to make a decision on his behalf right now. It would require a clear head and time to weigh what would be in Mark's best interest. Mark could either remain with Carla, if she was in agreement, or he could come to live with us but I just didn't feel I was in the position to make any major decisions at that time.

Suddenly, Carla piped up, "Oh, and by the way. I don't know if Sarah mentioned it to you or not but Matt, Jennifer and I have planned a trip to China. We're leaving next month on December 2. Sarah offered to take Mark with her while we were on vacation but now I don't know what we're going to do."

She was obviously hinting for us to take care of Mark while they were gone, so, I quickly answered.

"No problem, we'd love to have him stay with us."

With that being settled Carla returned to the topic of Sarah's house.

"You know, we're considering moving into this house. If we did we could move Mark's trailer from the back of our place and hide it over there behind the fence."

Hearing her talk about future plans for Sarah's house, two days after her death struck a deep chord of suspicion and left me feeling unsettled. Besides, what right did she have even entertaining thoughts like that when legally it wasn't Sarah's house yet? The house was still in Robert's name. In fact, it was Carla herself who said the papers hadn't been signed by Robert to transfer the house over to Sarah before her death. Sarah had been killed before anything was finalized but I was too distraught to make any sense of anything Carla was saying, so I just stood there listening to her ramblings.

"If we put the trailer behind the fence it would be out of sight and the municipality wouldn't even know anything's there. It would be a much better set up than what we have for him right now. The guys from the municipality are always driving by and they can see his trailer from the road."

When Doug pointed out it was still Robert's house, Carla just laughed and said,

"Ya, it's too bad Sarah couldn't have waited one more day until the deal was finalized. Oh well, we'll just have to deal with that when the time comes".

Disturbed by the callousness of Carla and Matt's attitude and their lack of compassion when they referred to Sarah, I was left not knowing what to think of it all. I just wanted to get out of there, so I motioned to Doug it was time for us to leave. I knew Sarah had named me as one of the beneficiaries in her will and I knew, as a beneficiary, I was entitled to have a copy of the will, so, before driving off I asked Carla if she would send it to me in the mail.

"No problem." She answered, "I'll mail out a copy to you right away."

We quickly let them know we'd be in touch regarding the funeral and to make arrangements for taking care of Mark while they were in China. Then, after spending a few minutes with Mark and giving him a lingering heartfelt hug we pulled out of the driveway. As we stopped before pulling onto the highway we were flagged down by someone, who judging by his swagger, was obviously quite drunk. Poking his head into the side window he blurted out, "You must be Sarah's sister! Glad to meet ya! Did ya git everythin' you guys was lookin' fer?"

Then, after poking his head even further inside the van, over beer-soaked breath, he offered his condolences before getting back into his truck and speeding off. We pulled away shaking our heads at his insolences, wondering who this character was and how on earth he knew why we were there. I looked at Doug and said,

"Small town, news travels fast, I guess." We both looked at one another and shrugged.

Self absorbed with sorrow, time seemed to stand still as we made our way down the highway.

~ Chapter Two ~

"When something bad happens you have three choices, you can either let it define you, let it destroy you, or let it strengthen you."
~ Unknown

It was well past midnight by the time we arrived home that evening. As usual the cats heard us pull into the driveway and were all anxiously waiting to greet us as we walked through the front door. The strain of dealing with the affairs of the past few days combined with the lengthy trip home left both of us drained and had taken us to the point of exhaustion. After refilling the cat dishes with food and giving them their treats, we literally fell into bed. As tired as I was, a stream of unsettling thoughts continued to race through my mind. I just couldn't ignore the red flags raised over the past few days and I was left to put an exerted effort into calming down the chaos running through my mind. Eventually, after hours of exhausting thought sleep did come.

The following morning I faced the dreadful task of contacting family and friends to tell them what we'd learned about the accident and discuss the funeral arrangements. It took everything I had to repeat the story of the fatal accident over and over again. When I finished making the final call I was totally depleted, so I made my way to the bedroom. As I passed by the computer I stopped to check my messages. There was one message waiting for me and as promised, a picture of Mark, in all his glory, all dressed up as Batman and ready to go shelling out. I managed a smile. Unsettled, overwhelmed and confused I continued down the hallway to try and steal a few moments of rest.

The more I tried to calm my mind the more my thoughts darted sporadically trying to make sense of the situation. The recent conversations with Matt and Carla continued to nag at me leaving me unable to find any sense of peace what so ever. Their whole demeanor reeked of disrespect and I couldn't shake the feeling something wasn't adding up. Sarah adored them both and made her feelings well-known but it was obvious there was a definite disconnect between Sarah's infatuation with them and their shameful attitude towards her. I have never been a fan of either of them but as I lay there thinking of the insensitivity they showed Doug and I and the disrespect they showed when they spoke of Sarah I was left confused. Because I was aware of their devious behavior in the past, I was left increasingly uncertain of their motives. With a heightened sense of suspicion I delved deeper into trying to make sense of it all and I found myself being taken on an agonizing search for the truth.

My immediate thoughts travelled back to the time of my brother's birth in March of 1955. Born and raised in Cambridge. I was only five years old when Mark was born so my recollection is vague but I do remember him being a great source of concern in our family. From the moment he arrived home from the hospital it was increasingly evident there was a problem with his physical and mental development. By the age of three, after extensive testing, the doctors diagnosed Mark as being 'mentally retarded'. My mom and dad were told the damage to his mental and physical development was caused by a long labor and poor judgment on the part of the doctor overseeing the birth. This combination resulted in his brain being starved of oxygen. When the diagnosis was made, my parents were sent home to deal with this incredible life-altering situation on their own. At that time, there were no specialized government workers, no respite associations and no financial aid, in fact, there were no support systems of any kind. You were left entirely to your own resources in dealing with raising a mentally-challenged child.

As a family unit we adjusted, each in our own way, to find the best way of handling the crisis situation we'd found ourselves having to deal with. After the diagnosis, mom was left carrying the full burden of guilt as she tried desperately to handle the many demands of bringing up a child with special needs. She constantly doted on Mark, day and night. This was partly due to his lack of abilities but I think mostly because of the self-blame and condemnation she harbored towards herself. On the other hand, Dad, in an attempt to avoid carrying his share of the burden, chose to distance himself from the situation, resulting in his excessive drinking. As for Sarah and I, we took up the slack by growing up with an ingrained sense of responsibility to protect Mark from the cruelties of the outside world.

The responsibility of being left to care for Mark coupled with the pressures of raising us girls and keeping the household going while dealing with an alcoholic husband proved to be too much for mom. As a result when Mark was three years old mom suddenly collapsed from fatigue and required complete bed rest. Realizing the complexity of the situation with my brother and my mom's inability to care for the family, doctors suggested that Mark be placed in an institution. They reasoned with my parents that people who are retarded were not understood or accepted by society. Incapable of defending themselves and considered misfits, they were the first ones to have a finger pointed at them when a crime was committed, resulting in many of them being wrongfully accused of crimes they did not commit. In addition, they were concerned about my sister and I suffering from neglect because of the amount of attention Mark would require. They also felt the stigma that society attached to siblings having a brother who is retarded would be detrimental to our mental health. Thus, the wheels were put in motion for Mark to be institutionalized.

From that moment on our home became completely void of joy. This life-changing decision hung heavy in the air, monopolizing every waking moment. Every conversation my parents shared resulted in mom retreating to her room only to return some time later, eyes red and swollen. As a child, with limited understanding of the scope of what was taking place or what was involved in being responsible for raising someone with mental disabilities, I just couldn't believe my parents were considering sending my brother away to live in an institution. I clearly remember trying to make sense of the insanity happening around me but always found myself coming back to the same state of hopelessness. After all, I was a child and had absolutely no say in the matter. Forced to stand by in disbelief, plans evolved and the day finally arrived for Mark to be sent away. Recalling the helplessness I experienced and remembering the devastation I felt for the loss of my brother is something that remains with me to this day.

The institution chosen for Mark to live in was called Cumberland Regional Center. Cumberland was a government facility built in 1915 on the outskirts of Barrie. Labeled the "Asylum for Idiots" this massive stone structure was erected to specifically accommodate the developmentally disabled. In order to remain in contact with Mark we would take the hour and a half drive to Barrie once a month to visit with him. As a kid, I remember how exciting it was while we were making plans for our monthly visits.

The anticipation of seeing him and spending time with him was always so much fun but at the end of the day, when it came time to say good bye, it was as if a shroud of sadness surrounded our family and remained there, until our next trip to see him the following month. Sarah and I were young at the time but we were well aware of the crippling effects this tragedy had on our lives.

Our monthly ritual continued until Mark was seventeen when the government began to shut down the large institutions and we were forced to seek other accommodations for him. At that point he was transferred from Cumberland, to a group home on Empire Avenue, in Cambridge. This allowed him the opportunity to work for ARC Industries, a government sponsored work shop, during the week and return home to live with mom and dad on weekends. For years this proved to be an ideal arrangement but it wasn't without its difficulties. Living in an institutional environment had taken its toll and left its mark on my brother. Unbeknown to anyone at that time, Mark had suffered at the hands of ruthless caregivers, while residing at Cumberland. Understandably, he was left dealing with deep-seated feelings of violation and abandonment, leaving him to sort through issues concerning anger and rage throughout his entire life.

In order to relieve her profound feelings of remorse Mom continued to set no boundaries for Mark. Throughout his early childhood and continuing into adulthood he was allowed to wreak havoc wherever and whenever he chose and as a result, much of mom's time was taken up trying to deal with his out-of-control temper. As I've already mentioned, Dad coped by alienating himself from the situation, choosing to spend much of his time with his drinking cronies rather than spending time with the family. Somewhere between all the chaos Sarah and I were left trying to sort through our own feelings of abandonment and struggled to find out where we fit into it all. Regardless of the disorder and confusion we all settled into our own distinctively dysfunctional roles and somehow life continued on. Mark remained living at Empire, Mom continued to dote on Mark, Dad kept drinking and Sarah and I grew up and branched out trying to make the best of things with what little guidance we'd been offered.

In the early '90's, Sarah was in the position to purchase a house close to where my girls and I lived. Shortly before her purchase, Mom and Dad made the decision to remove Mark from Empire and bring him home to try and care for him themselves. Although they tried, it didn't take long to realize that caring for Mark on a full time basis, at their age, was proving to be more than they could handle. This is when Sarah and I got together to brainstorm and figure out what we could do to help our parents. After much discussion we felt we had come up with a viable solution to help remedy this unexpected family situation and agreed to approach our parents to see how they felt about it.

We gathered everyone around the kitchen table and Sarah and I proudly presented our idea. Sarah offered to take Mark to live with her and my girls and I would rent an apartment in Sarah's house. We felt we'd come up with the ideal solution to help take care of Mark. With a little planning and rearranging of our schedules there would always be someone available to watch over him. The look of relief from Mom and Dad was all that was needed to set our plans in motion.

Within a short time, an adjacent two bedroom apartment was fixed up for the girls and I to rent from Sarah, and Mark made the move to live in one of her empty bedrooms. This arrangement allowed Sarah to continue to work because there was always someone available to keep Mark occupied and entertained. By now he was in his forties but he still required someone to keep an eye on him. We were brought up realizing Mark needed our support and protection so we had no problem in rearranging our lives to accommodate him.

As for my girls, there was no doubt they loved their Uncle Mark. Growing up with him they understood how vulnerable he was. At an early age they realized how much he depended on them so they were only more than happy to help in any way they could. It only seemed natural for us to band together, as a family, in order to meet Mark's needs. This living arrangement was not perfect by any means. Being a 'family affair' there were many ups and downs but nothing that couldn't be worked out. Mark just loved being part of the family and for his sake we just made it happen.

Over the next five years Sarah began breeding dogs and as her love of the breed grew so did her business. Eventually, she decided to leave her full-time job to focus on breeding the dogs and raising the puppies. Outgrowing her space was soon to follow. The puppies needed room to roam, so the search was on for the perfect place to establish her first kennel, as well as, space to accommodate her and Mark. After months of looking for a property that offered everything on her wish list she finally decided on a 25 acre hobby farm, just outside of Kingston. While the girls and I chose to stay behind and find a place of our own, Mark moved with Sarah when she relocated to their country home. The move went without incident and in July of 2000, filled with pride and excitement Sarah hung out her very first sign,

"Puppy Haven"
'The Home of Pampered Puppies'

Mark was fairly self-sufficient at this point so having a self-contained apartment for him, in their new home, was a bonus. The entire upstairs of the house fit the bill and became his personal domain. It contained a bedroom, a sitting room, a small kitchenette and a four-piece bathroom. Mark was capable of dressing himself, bathing himself, taking care of his personal hygiene and making simple meals and was absolutely thrilled about having his own space.

By nature he was outgoing and always wanted to be on the move. He had a personality that shined no matter where he went or who he met. Mark loved being around people and because of his wide range of interests there was never a lack of ways to entertain him. As long as I can remember, he enjoyed karaoke, the Leafs, Elvis, Batman, dancing, the Blue Jays, Terry Fox, fishing, listening to music, camping, watching TV, bowling, window shopping, going to the legion for a coke, and the list goes on. Mark simply loved life and enjoyed having fun.

Although Mark's speech is difficult to understand he somehow manages to get his point across. His most debilitating trait is his inability to understand the consequences of dangerous situations, making it necessary to have him under a watchful eye at all times. Once settled into their new surroundings Sarah found much of her time was taken up with getting the kennel established. This left little time to spare for caring for Mark and it didn't take long for her to see she needed to hire someone to watch over him. At that point she decided to place an ad for a caregiver in the local newspaper.

There were a number of responses to the ad but Sarah was quite impressed with one woman in particular who lived in the area. Her name was Ilka. She was a real firecracker and she hit it off with Mark right away. She freely included him in all her own family activities and made sure he was always available to attend his family events, but the best part of it all was the fact Mark loved to spend time with her. She had a real insight into what Mark's needs were and always made sure he was on the go. She was very good to Mark and things seemed to be working out well for a couple of years until, for whatever reason, Sarah found it necessary to dismiss her. Even though I asked, Sarah never did tell me why she let her go. I just had to trust that she had her reasons.

Almost immediately, another ad was placed in the local paper for another caregiver and shortly afterwards a woman who also lived in the area, answered the ad. Relieved to hear a response, Sarah set up a time to meet and discuss the details of the job with her. Excited by the outcome of the interview and after Carla and Mark had spent a 'play day' together, to acquaint themselves, Sarah called and without taking a breath told me how things went.

"You wouldn't believe it!" She began. "Her name is Carla. She's a single mom of three, two boys and a girl and just to make ends meet she drives school bus and holds a part time job doing some kind of work for the police department. She says because her boys are involved in all kinds of sports, she could start taking Mark to their practices and games. They normally go camping in the summer and are involved in all kinds of winter activities and she says it wouldn't be a problem to take Mark along with them, provided I would allow her to take him away, for a few days at a time. She enjoys karaoke, dances and bowling and on top of that she belongs to the Legion. After spending a day together, Mark came home and told me he really liked Carla and when I spoke to her after their outing she thought her and Mark really hit it off. So, I hired her. She almost sounds too good to be true, doesn't she? What do you think?"

"She does sound like a perfect match." I quickly added. "Let's keep our fingers crossed that she's the one. I'm really happy for you, Sarah. Now you'll be able to get back to focusing on the kennel."

As it turned out Sarah was very pleased with Carla and began calling me periodically to give me an update on her performance. I recall one conversation, in particular,

"Honestly, she keeps him so busy. She's got him on the go all the time and he just loves being with her. On top of that he's always coming home with little gifts she buys for him. Can you imagine? She buys them out of her own money. So far, he's brought home a couple of CD's, a watch, a radio and yesterday he even came home with a nice, little camera. I just can't believe how good she is to him!"

Although I did share in Sarah's enthusiasm of finding a good match for Mark I found it a little strange hearing about all the gifts he was coming home with but then again I thought Carla may have been just trying to win the two of them over with her generosity.

After hiring Carla, the whole family had an opportunity to meet her at a surprise party we held for Mark's birthday. We were all anxiously awaiting Mark's arrival when Carla walked through the doors with him. After the initial shouts of surprise and the enthusiastic activity surrounding the arrival of the birthday boy, things finally settled down. This is when Carla brought everyone's attention to the new, obviously very expensive down-filled jacket Mark was wearing, making it a point for everyone to know this was her gift to him.

After watching her express excessive pride in her generosity I was left again with the impression that something just wasn't adding up. It was very difficult for me to believe someone in her situation, a single mom with a family to take care of, would be at liberty to continually spend her money on gifts for a client she worked for, especially an expensive down-filled, designer jacket.

I searched the room to see if anyone looked as though they shared in my skepticism of Carla's grand entrance but it appeared as though no one seemed to think anything was unusual until I caught Doug's attention. I could see by his raised eyebrow we were thinking along the same lines. I joined him and together we sat back and watched as Carla reveled in the praise she was receiving for her extravagant gift. As the day progressed and the party got into full swing our doubts concerning Carla faded into the festivities but I can assure you they weren't forgotten.

About six months later, in the fall of that same year, while having a visit with mom, I happened to overhear Sarah explain how Mark went into a fit of rage one day while he was visiting Carla and smashed the glass in her patio door. Apparently, Carla couldn't afford to have it repaired and because it was Mark's fault to begin with Carla felt he should be the one to pay to have the damage fixed.

Mom thought things over for a moment then asked Sarah to find out what the cost would be to replace the glass. Sarah said Carla had already estimated it to be around fifteen hundred dollars. My chin dropped when I heard her quote the price. Personally, I found this estimate a little high to replace one piece of glass in a patio door but I was no expert, so I remained quiet as I watched mom go to her purse, pull out her check book and write out a check to Carla for the full amount. I was astounded.

A few weeks later, while Doug and I were having another visit with mom, Carla showed up to drop Mark off for the weekend. In an attempt to make small talk Doug asked her where she lived. She proceeded to tell him she's a single mom who lives with her three kids, not far from Sarah, in a house situated on a small parcel of land she received from her father. She said she'd been gradually fixing the house up for quite some time and commented on how nice it was to finally have a proper patio door installed after looking at a piece of plywood tacked up there all those years.

Doug nearly fell off his chair when he heard Carla's conflicting comment. He knew Carla blamed Mark for breaking the patio door and he also knew she'd been compensated, very well, for it. Now she was saying how nice it was to finally have a proper patio door to replace the plywood that had apparently been there for years. After he finished speaking with her he took me aside to tell me about the concerns he had regarding their conversation. He felt Mark may have been blamed for something he didn't do. After listening to what he had to say I agreed with him. As I sized up how her stories contradicted themselves I had no alternative but to conclude she had intentionally blamed Mark for something he wasn't responsible for in order to get the money from my mom. Although, that's exactly how it appeared I found it hard to believe someone could be that deceitful. Doug and I talked it over at great lengths but because we had no idea how to prove our suspicions, we decided to drop the subject and put the incident to the back of our minds.

Meanwhile, our own personal affairs were vying for our undivided attention. The kids were all out of the house by now and we were in the middle of relocating to a small town. We had discovered the perfect fixer upper in Fairport and were hoping to purchase it. Thrilled at the prospects of moving to an unfamiliar area and revamping an older house into our vision of the perfect home seemed to spark our sense of adventure. Once the papers were signed and we were settled into our new place it was time to acquaint ourselves with the advantages of small town living. We welcomed abandoning our ties with the hustle and bustle of the city but regardless of the distance we continued to remain involved with close family and friends we'd sadly left behind.

That year Mom suddenly became quite ill. It was a devastating turn of events, making it necessary for me to leave my peaceful existence and travel to be by her side to help with her care. It was the middle of October and with the help of the palliative nurses we managed to keep her as comfortable as possible as we watched her frail body deteriorate before our very eyes. During this unsettling time Doug would travel to be with me on weekends and return home to Fairport during the week.

This solemn time was marked by Sarah and Mark paying an unexpected visit to see mom on November 11. While I sat off to the side in the lazy boy I couldn't help but hear a conversation they were having together. Sarah was explaining to mom how Carla had eight hundred dollars stolen from her purse that she'd left on the school bus she was driving that morning to place Mark in the crowd to watch the Remembrance Day parade.

Apparently, Carla was on her way to the bank for an appointment with the manager and had eight hundred dollars cash with her so she could pay the mortgage. Sarah emphasized how devastated Carla was because she wouldn't be able to make her mortgage payment and didn't know what she was going to do. Sarah went on to tell mom that Carla felt it was Mark's fault the money was stolen because if she hadn't stopped to place him in the parade, the money would never have been taken. At that point I just couldn't sit back and not say anything. I could no longer contain myself, so, I piped up and asked Sarah if Carla had locked the bus door?

She turned to me and snapped, "I'm not sure. She was in a real hurry today so she might have forgotten to lock it."

"Well, don't you think she should take on some of the responsibility herself? If she was that stupid to leave her purse with that much money in it and forget to lock up the bus then I say she deserved to get robbed!" I blurted out.

Looking around the room I could see my personal opinion wasn't being received well by either mom or Sarah. None the less, I ignored their obvious disdain with my bluntness and merely asked, "Has she notified the police?"

Sarah quickly responded, "As far as I know she didn't. All I know is she's pretty upset about the whole situation. Anyways, it's true. If it weren't for having to place Mark to watch the parade in the first place it never would have happened at all."

Clearly, Sarah had sided with Carla and believed Mark was to blame for the whole incident and it was plain to see, as ill as mom was, she was once again left to take on the burden of guilt for Mark. From past experience, I knew I was facing a losing battle if I even suggested Carla take on any of the responsibility for the part she played. Realizing I was outnumbered, I once again sat back and watched while Mark was being blamed for something he wasn't responsible for.

Even though I knew what was being done to him was wrong I also knew how deep Carla's influence over Sarah went. I knew the influence Sarah had over mom and I knew how much guilt mom felt with Mark. I backed away from this situation knowing it was just too great a challenge for me to combat on my own. Realizing the impossible position I was in, I reluctantly let it go but secretly prayed for something to happen to prove Mark's innocence.

Later that evening, Doug and I talked about the stolen money. We both felt Mark's vulnerability was being taken advantage of by Carla. The sad thing is Mark didn't even realize what was going on. The longer we talked the more we began to recognize how much of Carla's story just didn't make sense. First of all, the banks aren't open on Remembrance Day, so it was unlikely she had an appointment with the manager at the bank that day. Secondly, we questioned why she would be carrying such a large sum of cash around with her but most importantly we wondered why she hadn't called the police to report the money being stolen? Already aware of her underhandedness in the past, this latest incident only served to help confirm our suspicions about her credibility. At that time, my attention was focused on caring for mom during her final days and as a result this latest incident with Carla was soon lost in all the emotional turmoil.

On November 30, 2004, mom passed away. After the funeral I remained at the house while Sarah and I, as co-executors, took care of dispersing Mom's estate. When Mom's final bank statement came in for November, I opened it and was shaken when I saw there was a cancelled cheque written out to Carla for eight hundred dollars and sure enough it was deposited on November 12. I just couldn't believe my eyes.

Suddenly, I began to seethe. All the unleashed anger I had concerning Carla's past behavior began to rise within me and I asked myself. *What kind of person does this? Takes advantage of the most unsuspecting and vulnerable? Mom, a widow on her death bed! Mark an innocent handicapped man! Neither of them deserved to be taken advantage of by this despicable woman who obviously had no morals or scruples.* That was the exact moment I dared to pass judgement on Carla and labelled her for what I felt she actually was; a liar and a thief!

In spite of the relentless feelings of loss I experienced after mom passed away, somehow, life continued on. Mom's belongings were distributed, the estate was dealt with and I was able to return home to Newport in April, where life began to take on a sense of normalcy for me. I felt bad leaving Sarah. She was having such a difficult time dealing with mom's passing. I promised her and myself I would keep close contact until she felt sure she was able to get on with her life. It was such a comfort for me to finally be back in my own house where Doug was fully engaged in renovations. Funny thing is, even with all the noise of nailing and sawing and all the mess of the sawdust and the inconvenience of everything being turned upside down, it felt so good to finally be home.

Then, unexpectedly, during the first week of June I received a very disturbing phone call.

As soon as I picked up I heard Sarah exclaim, "You won't believe what your brother has done now!"

And without a pause she continued,

"Carla had him out shopping today and he got caught shoplifting! Now they've charged her because she was with him. Do you know what this means? She's going to lose all of her part time jobs, driving school bus and definitely the job she has working for the detention center! That poor woman! I just can't believe this is happening!"

After taking a minute, to organize my thoughts, I asked if Mark had been charged with anything.

"No, he hasn't. They've charged Carla with using a handicapped man to shoplift out of Walmart."

"Well, don't you think if Mark was involved in any way they would have charged him too? He's not a child, you know." I pointed out.

"I don't know what the whole story is yet but I do know Carla wouldn't lie to me. She says it's all a big misunderstanding and hopes the charges will be dismissed. Anyways, if she says it was Mark's fault then it was his fault! I feel so bad for her. I told her I would pay for her legal expenses out of the trust money mom left to him."

Wondering if I'd heard her correctly, I asked, "Do you mean you're going to pay for all of her legal fees?"

"Of course I am. If it weren't for Mark, she wouldn't be in this mess in the first place!" Sarah snapped back.

I wonder where I've heard that before, I thought to myself before replying. "I think I'd want to know a little more about what actually happened before I committed myself to paying her legal fees." I added.

Sarah replied, "Well, her word is good enough for me. I just don't know what I'm going to do with Mark!"

I was left dumbfounded not knowing what to think of what I was hearing. I was very upset at how Sarah had become so loyal to Carla. It seemed she was just too quick to blame Mark and even quicker to agree with whatever Carla said. Again, I had a gut feeling something just wasn't adding up with what Sarah was telling me. By this time Carla had lost all credibility in my eyes and no matter what she said or did I think I would have been suspicious of her intentions. I knew Sarah didn't share the same opinion of Carla as I did and I also knew there was no sense in trying to point out anything that questioned her story let alone bring up anything that could possibly help to unfold the truth.

Once again, I felt my hands were tied because Sarah was the one responsible for making decisions, on behalf of Mark. When we had a difference of opinion there was nothing I could do but to have my say and let it be. Anyways, besides my suspicions I had no way of proving what really happened that day. I had no alternative but to stand by while Sarah insisted on condemning Mark for the theft and whole heartedly defended Carla's innocence.

Over the following year many of our conversations were centered on Carla's pending court case coming up in the spring. From what Sarah told me Carla was going to plead not guilty. Carla was sure once she had a chance to explain the misunderstanding that took place with Mark the judge would drop the charges. Sarah believed her and was adamant about covering the entire costs of Carla's legal fees. She said she felt indebted to Carla, not only because of the charges being laid against her but also the fact Carla had been put on suspension by her other employers and was in jeopardy of losing these jobs because of the charges. Sarah also felt Carla deserved some sort of compensation from Mark for all the embarrassment he had caused her. By now word of the charges had made their way into the local newspaper and around the community staining her reputation. As for Doug and I, we were not so fast in believing anything Carla said and preferred to wait for the verdict from the judge.

Totally amazed that Carla still wanted to continue to care for Mark, even after what he'd put her through, Sarah's gratitude towards Carla increased, leaving me not knowing what to think of it all, let alone what to do about it. Suspicious of how Carla victimized our ailing mother and how she takes advantage of Mark's naivety and vulnerability for her own financial gain severed any trust I may have had in her but I also realized I had no solid proof of her guilt. To add to my frustration, Sarah wasn't open to hearing anything I had to say about Carla, so for the time being I was forced to stand back, keep my thoughts to myself and just observe what was going on.

At long last, June 6, 2006, had arrived. This is the day Carla got to have her day in court. Today was the day we had all been waiting for, would she be found innocent or guilty of theft? I anxiously waited for Sarah to call with the answer. Around three in the afternoon the call came in. Picking up the phone I asked the question,

"Well, what's the verdict?"

"They found her guilty!" Sarah shrieked. "They've sentenced her to five years of probation and she's banned from all Wal-Mart stores for life, even though it's her first offense! More importantly, the judge didn't believe she was innocent. Can you imagine what that poor woman is going through right now? This is really going to affect her life. She'll never get her jobs back now, she'll have a record and once word gets around she'll never be able to hold her head up around town again but regardless of all that she says she still wants to work with Mark. What an angel she is. I can't tell you how upset I am with Mark right now!"

I sat there shaking my head and wondering to myself what it was going to take for Sarah to see through this woman's façade. Changing the subject, I asked,

"Did Mark have to testify?"

"No. He was here with me all day"

"What! I exclaimed. "You mean you didn't go to court with her?"

"No. I had to take some puppies to the vet today for their shots and Carla didn't want to take Mark with her, so, he stayed here with me."

"Weren't you interested in hearing what went on?"

"Not really. Carla already told me what happened."

"And you believe her?"

"One hundred percent, she wouldn't lie to me."

"And now that she's been found guilty? Do you still believe she's innocent?"

"Of course I do. Like she said it was all a big misunderstanding. It's just too bad the judge didn't see it that way."

"Well, if it was up to me, Sarah, I'd fire her. You need to look into this further. Something just isn't adding up here."

"Oh Robin, you're always so quick to judge." Sarah sharply accused.

"And you're pretty damn naïve if you believe anything that woman says."

"Well, I do!" She snapped back at me.

"I think you're making a big mistake Sarah but you seem to have made up your mind and I really don't want to argue with you about it anymore but I am entitled to have my own opinion." I concluded.

When I hung up I sat for a moment to try and make sense of what was going on. I was ready to wash my hands of it all but realized I had to stay connected for Mark's sake. He needed someone to be his voice and obviously from what I was seeing from Sarah's stand on everything, I was sadly the only voice of reason available for him.

Before mom passed away, it seemed only natural for Sarah to take over full responsibility of making all personal and financial decisions on Mark's behalf. After all, she was trained in working with the mentally disabled and she had been Mark's main caregiver for many years. Although she wasn't legally required to keep me informed of what was going on in Mark's life, she felt she had a moral obligation to keep me aware of his affairs. This resulted in her always asking my opinion on any major decisions that had to be made in his life.

Because of her educated expertise, I never questioned any decision she'd ever made, until now. It was becoming increasingly difficult to watch as she continued to ignore Carla's obvious deceitful behavior and as a result, wrongly persecute Mark. At least now, after knowing about the guilty conviction I was reassured that my opinion of Carla was correct and I felt justified in going against the grain and pointing out the obvious flaws I saw in Carla's twisted lies.

~ Chapter Three ~

"There are two things that one must get used to or life will become unendurable, the damages of time and the injustices of men."
~ Sebastien Roch Nicholas

Sarah had a good start on establishing the kennel by the time she met Robert. They met at a New Years Eve dance and seemed to hit it off right from the start. After dating for a short while it just seemed natural for Robert to move in with Sarah and Mark. Between them they shared in the running of the kennel and managed to keep things going quite well by themselves. By all appearances everything seemed to be going smoothly, until one day Sarah confessed to me she was overwhelmed with the ongoing stress and strain of running the business. Even with Robert's help, the daily chores of keeping up the kennel proved to be a daunting task for her to keep things moving forward. She said she was beginning to resent the fact that between Mark and the puppie, she never had a moment to herself. There was always something more to do just to keep up with things and although she loved Mark and her puppies, she was feeling defeated and totally drained.

This was the first time I heard the desperation in her voice and I understood completely why she would be feeling this way. To start with, the dogs and puppies had to be constantly maintained with never ending trips to the vet; there was breeding, monitoring the expectant mamas, sleepless nights spent whelping the puppies, cleaning up after them, feeding, weighing, bathing and brushing them. In addition, meticulous records of the blood lines had to be kept, advertising had to be dealt with and time had to be set aside for prospective buyers to come and see the pups. On top of that, she travelled extensively to world-class dog shows, winning many ribbons and trophies to bring home and display. No doubt she was exhausted. As she became increasingly weary it was noticeably reflected in her obvious indifference towards life in general.

Because of the lengthy four hour drive between us and the fact we were right in the middle of renovating our own bedraggled home there was very little Doug and I could do to lessen the load for Sarah. When we were there we did what we could. During one of our visits we managed to get Mark reconnected with the local legion. He was welcomed into the branch with open arms and shortly after becoming a member he was unofficially voted in as their "Official Greeter". He was very proud of his newly appointed position and loved to attend just to sit and enjoy a coke or two while greeting anyone who walked through the doors. As a result, each month we would make a point of visiting a couple of times to make sure he was able to attend the legion for an afternoon.

While staying at Sarah's I began to notice she was helping herself to a few more drinks than usual. I knew Robert and her were experiencing difficulties in their relationship, so I assumed her excessive drinking was the result and figured Sarah would get back to her old self again once things were worked out between them.

It wasn't long after that I began noticing the faint tinkling of ice cubes in the background during our evening conversations on the phone. Eventually, it got to the point where it didn't matter what time of day or night it was, those all too familiar tinkling sounds were ever present. When we'd be there visiting, I noticed her pouring drinks for herself earlier and earlier in the day. I tried to remain silent but one morning I decided to bring my concerns about her excessive drinking to her attention. Making light of it she merely laughed and casually said it was the only way she knew how to make it through the day anymore then quickly changed the subject. Avoiding answering my question was a clear indication to me that this was a bigger problem than what I'd originally thought.

My concern for Sarah resulted in us travelling to see her more often than usual. It was totally out of character for her to behave this way. Up until now she was strictly against drinking alcohol. She didn't like the taste of it, she didn't like the smell of it and she didn't like the way it made her feel. Sarah had always been headstrong, clear thinking and firmly grounded and that is what made this sudden change of behavior so puzzling. I felt being there for her and letting her know she had a soft place to fall was the answer. Unfortunately I was sadly mistaken, her drinking escalated and my heart broke for her.

Often, when we travelled to Sarah's we'd arrive to find out Carla had decided to take Mark out somewhere for the day. I never understood why she had to take him out every time we visited. She was quite aware that one of the main reasons for us traveling to Sarah's was to be able to spend time with Mark. After all, he was my brother and I didn't get to see him that often. When I'd mention this to Sarah she'd give Carla a call, asking her to bring Mark back home so we could spend some time together.

A short time later Carla would arrive with Mark and then she'd disappear to sit on a chair in the corner with her sunglasses on trying to appear aloof. Never once did she try to join in the conversation, making it a very uncomfortable situation. When she felt it was time to leave she would motion to Mark, then get up and out the door they'd go without her saying a word. I found her whole demeanor to be very odd but then again, my opinion of her was already stained with suspicion, so I don't know what it would have taken to get me to see her in a different light.

Over time I had come to dislike the woman, partly because I knew she was a liar and a thief and partly because I could see how she was manipulating and influencing Sarah and Mark. I started noticing how

Sarah would praise Carla for the most insignificant thing and was forever expressing her indebtedness to her. At the same time, it was obvious Mark was becoming increasingly dependent upon Carla for everything. It didn't matter what was said or asked of him he would look to Carla for the answer.

His stock replies to any questions were, "I don't know ask Carla." "I don't know, Carla knows." "Carla says no." "Carla says OK." "Carla says I can't."

It was quite evident Mark had lost the ability to have his own opinion on anything while his need for approval from Carla was made clear by his subservient demeanor towards her.

I tried to bring Mark's dependence on Carla to Sarah's attention a number of times but she would just shrug it off by saying, "The kennel has been taking up a lot of my time and Mark's been spending a lot of time at Carla's lately. It's only natural." She'd say, "Don't worry about it."

Then she'd always add, as if trying to convince me of Carla's virtuous motives,

"I really don't know what I'd do without her. She's an absolute angel."

Knowing Sarah's loyalty to Carla I had to pick and choose my words when trying to get her to see my point of view. I felt as if I was losing my brother and sister to the control of a stranger. I didn't understand it and couldn't explain it but the signs of manipulation were there. At this point it was just a gut feeling and I had to tread lightly when it came to pointing out anything negative about Carla to Sarah but there was definitely something wrong with this whole scenario. I felt helpless and was forced to muffle my feelings, for the time being.

Observing how worn out Sarah looked and seeing for myself the amount of time and energy that went into running the kennel, I offered to take Mark back with us for the summer. I no sooner got the words out when she jumped across the table and hugged me saying,

"Would you? You don't mind? That would be great! Then I could focus on what I have to do around here, instead of constantly worrying about what he's up to. Thanks for the offer. I'll get his stuff ready to go right now."

When Mark finally came into the room and was told he was coming to stay with us for a while, he became very excited. He'd always enjoyed visiting with us, so I began telling him about all the things we'd do while he was there. Our property backed on to the river which meant, with the weather warming up, he could go fishing and go with us when we went out in the boat. He really liked the idea of that and when I mentioned the picnics we'd have at Turner's Bay, his eyes lit up. Then he remembered the cats, he loved the cats. Now he was really worked up about going back with us. Actually, by the time I was finished telling him about all the things we would do during his stay I was beginning to get pretty excited myself.

Mark was packed and ready to go in no time and pretty soon we were heading down the highway towards home. It was a leisurely drive as we stopped for a number of breaks along the way to treat Mark to his favorite, McDonalds, for lunch and for dinner. It was late when we pulled into the driveway, so after I made up Mark's bed and he was settled in for the night we called it a day only to be woken up abruptly, the next morning, to the sound of a high pitched screech coming from a radio in Mark's room. Then, above the sound of the static we heard a rather gruff, slightly off tune voice, trying to keep up with Elvis singing "Jailhouse Rock". I put my housecoat on and thought I'd better see what this was all about. When I peeked into the bedroom, I noticed Mark was already dressed and sitting on the bed singing his heart out while trying to get the station tuned in clearly.

Going into the kitchen I could see he'd already eaten, then, I recalled Mark had always been an early riser with a strict morning routine. He would get up to have a bath around six, after his bath he brushed his teeth and shaved. Making sure the bathroom was left tidy he would return to his room to get dressed and make his bed and then he would go to the kitchen to make his breakfast; always a bowl of cereal, a piece of toast with jam and a glass of milk. When he finished eating he would clean up his dishes then return to his room and listen to his radio. This was his routine. It was the same day after day, never changing. It was sad in a way, to realize this behavior was the result of him being institutionalized for all those years and it brought up deep seated feelings of regret and guilt from deep within.

When I went into the room to tell Mark we'd be going shopping later that day he was thrilled. He immediately perked up and asked, "McDonald's?"

"Of course, McDonald's! Is there anywhere else?" I answered back sarcastically.

It didn't take long before he was waiting for Doug and me beside the van. Watching his exaggerated enthusiasm over going shopping, I smiled to myself and thought *it really doesn't take much to make him happy*. We enjoyed lunch at McDonald's first and then spent the afternoon window shopping. After picking up a few groceries we made our way towards home to prepare dinner. After helping to put the groceries away Mark decided to sit on the side patio and listen to his radio. Doug and I joined him once dinner was ready and while we ate he excitedly pointed out every time a boat passed by on the river. Later that evening, Doug decided to give Mark a haircut out on the back deck. Mark was pleased with the results, indicating it reminded him of Elvis's hair.

One of the many things Mark enjoyed doing was watching movies and sports on TV. Sarah had supplied him with his own TV in his apartment and had hooked him up with The Sports Network and The Movie Channel, allowing him to watch whatever he wanted whenever he liked. Because we weren't hardcore TV watchers, we only had one television in the whole house and we didn't subscribe to any special channels. Mark just couldn't comprehend why he wasn't able to watch his sports or settle in to watch a movie whenever he wanted to. No matter how many times we tried to explain this to him, he just wasn't able to understand why his favorite shows weren't available. When he was able to find a program he was interested in watching he demanded absolute silence in the room. Any noise of any kind usually ended up with him becoming very agitated, retreating to his room and slamming the door behind him. This resulted in the household being in a constant state of frustration.

In an attempt to settle the problem of this continuous disruption over the TV, we decided to move our small travel trailer up beside the house, where we could plug in electricity and run water to it. This would give him his independence while allowing us to keep a close eye on him. We put a small TV and VCR on the counter of the trailer and rented him a ton of movies to watch. Mark thought this setup was all quite amusing and liked the idea because he said it was, "just like camping". This arrangement allowed him to come and go as he pleased. He had the option of either having his meals in the house with us or taking them out to the trailer. The choice of either sleeping out in the trailer or coming inside and sleeping in his bedroom was entirely his choice. The important thing was; he had choices.

Pleased with how well our visit was going, I called Sarah to let her know about Mark having access to the trailer. Mark referred to it as 'my own place' and loved having his privacy while he was out there. There was even a tiny fridge to keep his drinks and pudding cups cool and cupboards to store his goodies in and because it was situated by the front door we felt secure in knowing we were close enough to keep a good eye on him. We felt it was the ideal solution.

One morning after spending the night in the trailer and after having his bath Mark announced he was going to eat his breakfast in his own place. Figuring he would just lie down and listen to his radio afterwards, Doug and I lingered over our morning coffee, discussing our plans for the day. After about an hour we were startled when a police car pulled into the driveway. I hurried out to see what was going on and was surprised to find Mark sitting in his lawn chair on the opposite side of the trailer where we couldn't see him. He was at the side of the road waving his Canada flag and cheering a crowd of kids on as they jogged past the house. Cluing in, I realized today was the day of the Terry Fox Run and when I noticed the officer walking towards Mark it became plain to me we had a problem on our hands. I could see this scenario was heading towards disaster and it had Mark's name written all over it.

When Mark noticed the policeman coming his way, he ran up to greet him. Patting him on the back he asking him enthusiastically,

"You a pwiceman?"

When Mark noticed me coming towards them he started nodding his head while affirming to me,

"Wobin, Pwiceman my fwend! Pwiceman my fwend!"

I couldn't help but smile at the obvious sense of pride Mark displayed towards the men in uniform who upheld the law and I replied,

"You're right Mark. The policeman is your friend!"

As I reached the back of the trailer, I approached the officer and asked,

"May I help you?"

The officer began by asking if I knew this man and after letting him know he is my brother, he told me there had been a complaint about him by one of the teachers at the school. Reading the expression on the officer's face, I could see he had caught on to Mark's childlike behavior as he continued to tell me about the complaint. He went on to explain, it was the day of the annual Terry Fox run at the local public school and all the teachers and kids were participating in it by running and the run was scheduled to go right past our place. When one of the teachers arrived back at the school they complained to the principal about an old man sitting at the side of the road along the route yelling obscenities to the kids, something about his hair. Immediately, the officer's eyes looked downward to indicate pubic hair but more importantly he stressed the principal was particularly upset by the fact Mark was taking pictures of the kids with his camera. I stood there speechless to think Mark was being portrayed as some kind of pervert. It was ridiculous to think there was any sort of sexual motivation behind his actions.

I gasped, "Oh My God, I can't believe this!"

Turning to Mark for an explanation I noticed a camera hanging from his neck.

"Mark, what on earth have you done?"

"No my fault, Wobin! No my fault!" He shouted again and again in his defense.

Turning to the officer I blurted out,

"I honestly don't know what to say about any of this. It's just not like him. I hope you can see he meant no harm. I'll contact the school and deal with this immediately."

Trying to get a handle on what was happening I took a moment to gather my thoughts and try to make sense of the situation but in order to do this I had to put myself into Mark's mode of thinking, so I tried to reason. *I could understand that Mark would have recognized the familiar logo on their t-shirts as they jogged by and I could understand why he decided to enthusiastically cheer everyone on because Terry Fox was one of his all time favorite heroes but to accuse him of yelling obscenities? I honestly don't know how anyone could even make out what he was saying, let alone accuse him of throwing out comments of a sexual nature. Mark was extremely difficult to understand, even at the best of times.*

And as far as him taking pictures? I could see him taking them because the Terry Fox Run was one of his favorite events but not for the seedy reason they were making it out to be; a dirty old man getting pleasure out of snapping pictures of young children. No way, that wasn't Mark. He had the mind of a child and I quickly realized this was one of those times my mom had been warned about by the doctors and I knew I had to get to the bottom of things fast. I had to figure out exactly what took place before everything got out of control.

The officer broke into my line of thinking to say he would have to confiscate the camera, so I asked Mark to hand it over to me. It was an old Brownie and when I opened the back, to remove the film we looked at each other and started to chuckle. Apparently, Mark had been taking pictures with no film in the camera. The officer, at that point, could see the innocence of it all and said not to worry he would speak with the principal himself. As he turned to leave he removed his cap for a moment, revealing his hair. When Mark saw the officer's brush cut he ran up to him and began running his hand over his own freshly cut hair, saying,

"See? New hair cut. Doug cut nice for me. Same as you, just like Ellis Pwesley."

This was not the first misunderstanding I'd been through with Mark and I knew we hadn't heard the end of this, so once the officer left, we took Mark into the house to try to find out exactly what had gone on. We had no sooner sat down with Mark at the kitchen table, to try to sort through what had taken place earlier when the phone rang. It was my daughter, so I left Doug to continue talking with Mark while I discussed the incident with her privately. While I was talking to her I could hear Mark in the kitchen emphatically repeating to Doug,

"Sorry Doug! No my fault! Sorry!"

"I'm sure he has no idea of what he did wrong but it's going to be awfully difficult to figure this all out." I explained to my daughter. "There's no telling what the school might do if I don't get a handle on it soon.

This could end up having terrible consequences for him, especially if someone decides to lay charges."

Just then Mark came to ask if he could talk to his niece. I handed the phone to him and immediately he began telling her about his new haircut. He was so proud of the haircut Doug had given him the day before.

"Nice hair, just like Ellis Pwesley!" he exclaimed to her.

Suddenly, it hit us both at the same time as we hollered into the phone. "Of course, that's it! He was trying to tell the kids about his new haircut, just like Elvis Presley!" I let out a sigh of relief. As soon as we finished our conversation, I called the school asking to speak with the principal. Now that I had figured out an explanation for Mark's behavior I felt he deserved to have a voice in all the accusations that were being thrown at him. Once the principal came on the line I explained to him I was the sister of the man surrounding all the commotion earlier that day, suddenly he cut me off to point out his stern view of the situation,

"I just want you to know that once the children went home at noon today and they'd had a chance to speak with their parents I had some enquiries about the situation and felt I should at least give them an explanation to make them aware of what took place with your brother, so I sent them all home with a note this evening explaining what happened, according to what I had been told by the teacher. After all, I am responsible for the wellbeing of every child in this school and if someone poses a threat or is out there harassing them, in any way, I have to take whatever steps are necessary to protect them."

Appalled by his arrogance I tried to get the point across that my brother was mentally handicapped and in my opinion I didn't feel he'd ever at any time been a threat to the kids. I informed him I felt it was all a big misunderstanding and I thought everyone had been a little too hasty in their judgment. I told him I was hoping to speak with him personally, to clarify what had actually taken place and in doing so clear my brother's name of any wrongdoing. We made arrangements to meet at 4 pm the following day.

Not wanting to be late for our appointment we arrived early. While sitting on the bench waiting to be called into the principal's office I took a moment to wonder what Mark's perception of this whole sordid situation was. It was terrible how his actions were continually being misunderstood by people who are ignorant of those with mental disabilities. Unable to verbally defend himself or even understand the magnitude of the allegations he was accused of made it difficult for me to stand back and say nothing. People who don't understand the mentally disabled are frightened of Mark and view his behavior as threatening or as in Carla's case, see his vulnerability as something to be taken advantage of. I get very upset when I think of how terrible it must be for him to go through life being used because of his naivety and wrongly accused of things done in innocence.

Actually, it was the ignorance of the teacher's perception that gave a sexual tone to Mark's actions when she reported the incident. The truth of the matter was; it was all done in innocence. Mark was just being Mark. How quick people were to jump to conclusions when it came to him, judging him from a place of their own corrupt minds. I can't tell you the number of times, over the years, I had to jump in after seeing a store clerk try to short change him after a purchase or how many times, over the course of his life, I had to protect him when I saw someone lording their power over him as Mark stood there confused and defenseless. It was shameful!

Eventually, we were escorted into the office and after introductions, Mark, almost in tears, began repeating,

"Sorry, no my fault. Sorry!"

I leaned over and reminded him he had nothing to be sorry about.

"You have done nothing wrong Mark." I whispered.

Looking at the principal sitting poker faced behind his desk I could see how uncomfortable he was with Mark sitting across from him, so I began.

"As I mentioned to you before, Mark is mentally handicapped and he is down here visiting with us for the summer. What took place yesterday was all a big misunderstanding and I feel you and your staff were too quick to judge him, before you knew all the facts."

I looked at him sitting across from us, still pokerfaced and looking very uncomfortable by this time, so I continued,

"Mark is probably the least threatening person you will ever meet. What the teacher thought as him making sexual comments to the children about his pubic hair was actually him telling them about the new haircut he is so proud of and as far as him taking pictures of the kids, there was no film in the camera, there were no pictures. He wasn't out there gawking at the kids he was out there rooting them on. He knew it was the Terry Fox Run and Terry Fox is one of Mark's favorite idols. I think you jumped to conclusions yesterday, by alarming the parents about what happened and insinuating Mark was some kind of predator."

Ignoring anything I had just said he asked, "So exactly what would you like me to do about it?"

I jumped back in. "Well, for starters, I feel you should send home another notice explaining the truth to the parents and I believe you and the teacher who made the complaint owe Mark an apology."

He suddenly broke from his poker face and began staring at us with contempt, then he pointed out there was no way that was ever going to happen. He continued on by saying his responsibility lay with the safety of the children and it was best if we just forget about the whole situation. Then, looking directly at Mark he added,

"By the way, is he going to be visiting you often?"

"I can't say for sure how often but yes he will be visiting again, at some time"

Continuing to stare at Mark he stated,

"Well then, we'll have to make sure we change the route of the run for next year."

Shocked at his insolence and lack of compassion we immediately got up and left without saying a word. At that moment, I had to query if there had been any change in people's thinking during the past 50 years since the time Mark was sent away to live at Cumberland. Part of the reason he was institutionalized was because of the way society shunned people with mental disabilities. *Had anything really changed?* I questioned. As we walked down the hallway, I remembered the insolent words spoken by the principal and wondered, *how a man of his standing, responsible for so many children, could be so insensitive and narrow minded and I questioned his position as a role model for such influential minds.*

People's reaction to Mark never failed to amaze me. It saddened me to realize how things really hadn't changed in all this time and I've been left to wonder if they ever would.

~ Chapter Four ~

"It is during our darkest moments
we must focus to see the light."
~ Aristotle Onassis

Summer was beginning to wind down and it was time to think about returning Mark to Sarah's care. We were thoroughly enjoying our visit with him, so when he asked to stay a little longer, we didn't hesitate to call Sarah to ask if he could remain with us for a few more weeks.

"I don't mind," she said, "but Carla's been saying how much she misses him and wants him back home soon".

After pausing to consider Carla's request I continued to prompt Sarah until she finally agreed to him staying a little longer. I was pleased to hear she was allowing him to stay regardless of what Carla wanted and when I told Mark the latest news of an extended visit he jumped for joy. I knew our time together was coming to an end soon, so each day we were kept busy making sure to catch up on everything we'd planned on doing while he was here.

The following week Sarah called to tell me she'd purchased a small travel trailer and had it set up beside the house, ready for Mark when his vacation was over. We'd talked many times, over the summer, about how well it was working out with Mark having the trailer to spend time in and we both agreed this set up suited his needs perfectly. I was a little sad when we hung up because I knew when I told Mark what was in store for him his stay with us would be short lived. Sure enough, as soon as I mentioned Sarah had purchased a trailer for him and it was ready and waiting for him when he returned home, he was ready to end his vacation.

Before the week was out we were on the road taking Mark back home. As we reached our destination and pulled onto Sarah's driveway Mark saw the trailer sitting there, he was absolutely thrilled. He could hardly control himself and barely stayed in the van long enough for us to come to a complete stop before jumping out and running over to his 'new home'. Once inside the trailer he anxiously moved from room to room, opening every door and drawer, showing us where he planned to store away all his belongings. Standing back and watching how excited he was we were reassured about it being a wise purchase for him. Keeping our fingers crossed, we hoped he would begin to enjoy a sense of freedom and independence by having some personal space of his very own. After Mark finished showing us around we went to the house to let everyone know we'd arrived and to freshen up before dinner.

Once we entered the house it didn't take long to realize this was going to be a very trying weekend.

Sarah and Robert were battling with each other and you could have cut the tension in the air with a knife. The unpleasant remarks they exchanged towards each other left us feeling uncomfortable and made it impossible to relax and enjoy their company. From what I could gather Robert was upset and felt threatened because of Matt and Carla's interference in running the kennel, as well as their constant intrusion into his and Sarah's relationship. The real problem lay in the fact that Sarah didn't exactly see things that way. She felt they were just a very caring couple trying to be helpful but with my past knowledge of Matt and Carla's devious ways I was inclined to question their motives and I had to agree, Robert had every right to feel threatened.

At last, the weekend had come to an end and while I was busy packing our things up to leave Sarah came into the room. She apologized for all the unpleasantness between her and Robert and hoped we'd been able to enjoy ourselves regardless. While crossing my fingers behind my back I reassured her we'd had a great time. Then, boldly I stepped out of my comfort zone and took a chance by telling her it would be a shame if she allowed Carla to drive a wedge into their relationship. I could see by her reaction I'd struck a chord as she suddenly became defensive and told me Matt and Carla were absolutely indispensable to her. Then, she went on to say they helped her immensely and she didn't understand why people couldn't see that. I felt I had to bite my tongue before I said something I might be sorry for. I didn't feel Sarah would be able to handle the truth of how I really felt about them and besides I didn't want to allow them to come between the close relationship Sarah and I had between us. That was the last thing I needed, so I gave her a warm hug, told her I was just concerned about her and wanted to make sure she wasn't being taken advantage of.

We gathered our suitcases and packed them in the van then went to say good bye to Mark in his trailer. It was obvious he was busy setting up house as he filled the fridge with pop and pudding cups and crammed his clothes into the drawers. Saying goodbye to him was hard but at the same time I could see he was happy to be home. Uncertain about leaving him there to contend with all the friction going on between Sarah and Robert I consoled myself by knowing he had a private place of his own to go to if he needed some peace and quiet. Once we said our final goodbyes we were off, heading down the highway towards home. With Mark gone life would seem so uneventful but what a wonderful feeling it was when hours later we finally fell into our own bed!

The next morning, concerned over the obvious discord the weekend had presented, I couldn't get Sarah out of my mind. The vision of how tired she looked plagued me. The condition of her relationship with Robert was troubling but what bothered me the most was the influence and control Matt and Carla had over her. I just didn't understand the loyalty Sarah had towards them, after all, they were simply employees she hired to help her out and I'm sure she was paying them well. She really didn't owe them anything more than a paycheck.

I couldn't help but think something was terribly wrong with Sarah. From the moment we arrived until the moment we left she drank nonstop. I knew she enjoyed a drink now and then but this was different. This was from the time she got up in the morning until the time she went to bed at night. It just wasn't like her to drink like this and it hurt me to see her life in such disarray. If the time we spent with her over the past few days was any indication of her usual consumption of alcohol, I'd say, her drinking was definitely out of hand.

Once the leaves fell and the snow and ice began to cover the roads it became too treacherous for us to travel and we weren't able to visit Sarah as often as we would have liked, so we had to make do with regular contact through emails and phone calls. It appeared the long cold winter was taking a toll on Sarah. Her drinking rose to a whole new level and it broke my heart to hear her intoxicated and slurring her words every time we spoke on the phone. At this point, Robert was very concerned about Sarah's condition and would call us periodically to keep us informed of how things were going. Each call was more alarming than the last as her drinking escalated along with her dependence on Carla. I felt bad for Robert as he hopelessly tried to explain what was going on in their lives.

Robert felt he was slowly being squeezed out of Sarah's life. Most of his responsibilities to do with the kennel had been turned over to Matt and Carla. In addition, most days Sarah wasn't capable of driving or going anywhere in public because of her drinking. She was now dependent on them to do her banking and shopping. Robert was very upset as he explained to me how Sarah had just recently handed the books for the business over to Carla after she offered to keep them for her, adding at the same time that Matt had been given full signing authority over Mark's monthly disability check. I was horrified and Robert was at his wits end. Sarah seemed to be out of control and we didn't know how to get a handle on things. We just couldn't believe how Sarah was slowly handing their lives over to them, bit by bit. I sat there barely able to comprehend Sarah's destructive behavior as I listened to what he was saying. During our recent calls I'd heard the change in Sarah for myself. Disturbed by it all, I simply didn't understand the excessive trust and loyalty Sarah showed towards Matt and Carla. Sarah remained oblivious to any deceit or wrong doing on their part. I really didn't know what to make of what was going on but it laid heavy on my mind and I could only hope Sarah would come to her senses soon.

Robert and I kept in close touch for the duration of the winter and from what I gathered from our conversations Sarah remained dependant on Matt and Carla as Robert continued to be pushed out of the picture. Confused over the whole situation I was left with a feeling of impending doom. I just couldn't see any good coming out of any of it and I felt helpless. The winter season was merciless that year, never ending and extremely cold. What a relief when the snow finally melted, everything warmed up and spring finally arrived in all its glory. One day after coming in from working in the garden the phone rang, it was Sarah. We talked for a while catching up on all the latest happenings in our lives when she suddenly changed the subject and asked,

"What do you think about me moving Mark's trailer over to Carla's place?"

I was taken aback by her question and didn't quite know how to respond to it but I do know I didn't care for where this conversation was heading, so I asked her why she would do that and listened as she continued,

"When Mark's here he has his own space either upstairs or in his trailer but when he's at Carla's the conditions are not exactly ideal."

"What do you mean they're not exactly ideal?" I questioned.

"Well, they have a bed set up for him in the basement under the stairs but because their house is a split level, when anyone comes in the front door it's very noisy and if he's asleep he gets woken up. You know how they like to party and some nights the noise continues all night long. Even during the day, if he wants to lie down there's always people coming and going making a lot of noise and he gets agitated."

This was all news to me. I'd never been to Carla's house, in fact, we'd only met a handful of times but I was under the distinct impression Mark had a proper room to stay in when he stayed overnight there. As much as I wanted to question Sarah's judgment in allowing him to stay with Carla under those conditions, I held my silence and listened as she explained further.

"On top of that, quite often Matt and Carla take Mark along with them when they go out for the evening and after they've had a few drinks she doesn't want to take the chance of getting pulled over by the cops while driving Mark home. You know Matt already lost his license on account of a DUI charge and they certainly couldn't afford to have Carla lose hers too."

I took a minute to collect my thoughts before I asked,

"Isn't there some other arrangements that could be made besides moving his trailer over there?"

"Not really." She replied. "Carla and I have already talked it over and she says they could set up the trailer in their driveway so Mark would be able to sleep in it and still have easy access to the house if he needed to use the washroom or come in for meals. Ideally, he could choose to spend time out there or come inside if that's what he wanted. Carla says they would hook the trailer up to electricity so he'd have use of the refrigerator and be able to listen to his radio. They are even going to put in satellite TV so he would be able to relax and enjoy his shows while he's out there. That way he wouldn't be constantly irritated by the noise in the house. Actually it would be set up exactly the way we have it set up here. What do you think?"

Confused about what to think of this latest development but given the choice of Mark being kept up all night or having a quiet, restful place to sleep when he was at Carla's or having him driving home in the car when Carla was drinking or staying there where he would be safe I felt I had no choice but to agree with Sarah's idea. Sarah sounded pleased when I agreed with her but the truth be known, I felt I was forced to agree with the lesser of two evils.

A week later Sarah called to let me know Mark's trailer was all hooked up at Carla's and everything was working out great. After talking for a while she happened to mention Canada Revenue had sent her a letter letting her know she had been put on notice. They were preparing to do an audit on the books for the kennel. As far as I knew Carla was keeping the books for her and I figured Sarah wouldn't have handed them over to her if she didn't figure Carla was capable of doing them properly. I just assumed everything was in order. That's why I was surprised to hear Sarah say she was nervous about the upcoming audit. She broke into tears when she told me how afraid she was of the government delving into her finances. She knew she was in big trouble. Hearing this sent chills down my spine as I tried to console her. I found out later from speaking to Robert that her books were in an absolute mess. Apparently, Sarah and Carla had just spent weeks pouring over endless receipts and numbers trying to minimize the appearance of the ill-managed bookkeeping before the auditor arrived.

Sarah and I had many phone calls over the following weeks while the auditor was there. From what I could tell it was a grueling process that lasted more than three weeks and by the time he put down his pen and tallied up the damage, Sarah was charged with negligence and it ended up she owed over sixty-thousand dollars in unclaimed taxes. This latest incident caused her drinking to sky rocket and I was left not knowing what to say or do to help her deal with the situation. It was pitiful to watch as she agonized over how she was going to pay all this money back. Through this whole process I was bothered by the fact that, even though Carla was responsible for keeping track of the books it was Sarah who was left carrying the ball and although it was Carla's incompetence that was under the microscope, she was able to just walk away unscathed. I was livid at how Sarah was just letting this woman get away with everything and how she continued to talk about her as if she was a saint.

I agonized over the state my sister was in until the day I picked up the phone and surprisingly Sarah was on the other end sounding rather optimistic. She was really excited and couldn't wait to tell me how she'd figured out a way she could pay back her debt to the government. I sat and listened as she told me what she'd come up with,

"Just after Robert and I got together he bought a little two bedroom house situated not far from here near the village of Hampton and he's been renting it out ever since. It's really quite cute but he's only been asking enough in rent to keep the place going without costing him anything and the renters haven't taken very good care of it, so it does seem to have lost its luster and will probably require some work to bring it back to life but I figure if I sell the house we're living in now we'd probably end up with enough to pay off the sixty thousand dollar debt I owe to the government and there would still be ample left over to fix up the house in Hampton for us to live in. Even though the place isn't set up for a kennel I think the garage could be converted. I really think its doable Robin. What do you think?"

Amazed at her ingenuity I replied, "Wow Sarah! Go for it! Sounds like you've come up with the answer to your prayers."

It was so refreshing to hear her making plans for the future again. I think she had almost given up on being able to have any kind of future with the huge debt she had been saddled with. But her enthusiasm returned as she proceeded to sell her house and began making plans to fix up the little rental in Hampton. Within a few months she was able to pay off her debt to the government in full and was free to begin rebuilding her future. Her vision began to materialize when she hired a contractor to renovate the garage into a working kennel to house the dogs and puppies. A short time later the entire house was under construction. What a relief to see Sarah in charge of her life once again.

Finally I was able to put my concerns about her to rest and focus on my own life, until one afternoon shortly before the house was ready for them to move into Sarah called and laid another unexpected bomb on me. She wanted me to know she was going to purchase a one bedroom mobile home for Mark to replace the small travel trailer he'd been living in while staying at Carla's place. She was going to purchase it by withdrawing money from Mark's trust and have it placed at the far end of Carla's property so he could stay there permanently. My jaw dropped, I just couldn't believe what she was saying. Feeling confused, I prodded her for an explanation,

"What on earth for? Why would you do something like that?" I blurted out.

"Well," she began, "the house we're in now is only a two bedroom and there's just not enough space to accommodate the three of us. The second bedroom is so tiny it doesn't give Mark the room he needs and Carla has offered to have him stay at her place full time if we buy a proper trailer for him to live in. Her offer is very generous and I think I'll take her up on it. With the renovations going on he's been over there a lot lately anyways. Besides, I'll always make sure he has a place to stay here when he wants to visit and he'll be able to come home whenever he pleases."

My head was spinning as I replied "Well, I sure didn't see that one coming, Sarah."

I was really against the idea of Mark living at Carla's full time. *He's just too vulnerable to be left under her complete and constant control* I thought in horror. *He'd be defenseless against her constant evil influence.*

Suddenly, a horrible thought occurred to me, "You're not thinking of signing guardianship over to her, are you?" I asked.

"Of course not, you know I'd never do that. Her idea just seems like a good solution to the situation right now." She replied. "But I really don't know what to do with the trailer he's staying in now. If I put it up for sale I'd only get peanuts for it so I think I'm going to just give the little travel trailer to Matt and Carla for their own personal use. They like to camp a lot in the summer. So, what do you think?"

I hated it when Sarah asked me what I thought because I was always put in the position of being the devil's advocate and in reality what I thought didn't amount to a hill of beans. I had no authority to have an impact on anything to do with Mark. But I felt I had to give her my input in hopes she might begin to lean towards my way of thinking, unclouded by the unwarranted gratitude she had for Matt and Carla.

I took a deep breath, then replied, "OK, here's what I think, first of all, as far as Mark living there permanently, you know there's no love lost between Carla and me, so as far as that goes I have my reservations about him moving there but I guess if that's the only solution you can come up with I have no choice but to go along with you. Secondly, as far as you giving them Mark's old travel trailer I think you have given them far too much as it is but I'm not even going to bother trying to sway you in regards to that because you don't listen to me anyway and I know if you've got your mind set on giving it to them that's exactly what you're going to do."

Sarah indicated she'd taken my comment as being in agreement with her and just continued on,

"There's just one thing I should tell you, they can't hook the trailer up permanently to electricity or plumbing until they see how the municipality reacts to it sitting in their back yard. There's a bylaw in their area that states they can't have an occupied trailer on their property. Sometimes the town just turns a blind eye but Carla wants to give it some time to see what they're going to do. They don't want to put all the time and money into digging trenches for plumbing and extending wires for electricity, if by chance, the municipality did have a problem with Mark living there."

"Everything sounds pretty shady to me." I pointed out to her.

Sarah just laughed and told me everything would be just fine. Regardless of her positive attitude towards this move I was left with serious concerns about the repercussions of Mark residing with Carla permanently. I was finding it difficult to shake the feeling that this move would give Carla the leverage she needed to completely embed herself into their lives. Even though I made it clear I didn't care for this latest decision involving Mark's future, a large mobile home was bought using money from Mark's trust and placed right behind the pig sty at the far end of Carla's property just in time for Sarah to move into her newly renovated home.

Not long after Mark was settled into his new trailer I received another unexpected call from Sarah. She'd been drinking quite heavily and I found her extremely difficult to understand but through her slurred mutterings I managed to make out the gist of what she was saying. Apparently, Carla wanted to travel to Arizona with a friend but couldn't obtain a passport because of her conviction of theft, so Sarah decided to give her the money from Mark's trust to pay for a pardon.

"After all, if it weren't for Mark she would never have been convicted of stealing in the first place." She told me in an attempt to justify her actions.

My mind was reeling as I began to understand full the impact of what she was telling me and I was furious. Not able to think straight I ended our conversation quickly and sat in the silence trying to make sense of things. *How convenient for Carla! After all these years, she was still taking advantage of Mark and blaming him for her conviction. She had Sarah totally convinced of her innocence and now Mark was paying for her pardon.* I was convinced this woman was not going to give up until she had sucked every penny she could from this family. It just wasn't right but I knew anything I would say to disagree with Sarah's decision would be pointless. I had to take time to get a grip on my thoughts and then I planned to call her back to let her know, for what it was worth, how strongly I disapproved of what she was planning to do.

The following day after hearing from Sarah, Robert called. Clearly he needed someone to vent to. He was ranting because he'd just found out Sarah was sending Matt and Carla away for an exclusive all-expense paid weekend at St. Anne's Spa and apparently she was going to pay for it out of Mark's trust fund. I resented the fact Mark's trust was being used as a pacifier for Matt and Carla and I could hear the anger and frustration in Robert's voice as he made it plain he had absolutely no tolerance for either of them. I shared in his frustration and we both agreed they were well aware of the existence of Mark's trust and wouldn't be content until they'd depleted it of every penny. We both knew Sarah's excessive drinking coupled with the unfounded indebtedness she felt she owed the two of them made it easy for them to exploit her and they knew it.

As we continued to talk he told me how he witnessed them taking advantage of Sarah by feeding her drinks until she wasn't able to stand up and then ask her to hand over money to them for work they'd already been paid for. He went on to say what upset him the most about the whole situation was that Sarah just didn't see through any of their scams and wouldn't listen when he tried to tell her what they were doing to her. I was upset but not surprised at what Robert was telling me and I could totally relate to how he was feeling. He was no match for their constant bullying and it must have been agonizing for him to hopelessly stand by and watch as they slowly chipped away at consuming Sarah and Mark's lives, not to mention them doing their best to ruin their relationship. I told him I'd already heard from Sarah about the pardon and I was planning to speak to her later in the week. I was hoping to get her to see what the pair of them were up to but I didn't hold much hope in getting her to change her mind about what they were scheming.

After hanging up I realized I had to make the call to Sarah right away. Without hesitation I dialed her number and before I had time to tell her what I called for she began telling me about her decision to send Carla away for a well deserved vacation. It was hard for me to believe the excitement she expressed as she went into great detail about the arrangements she's made for their little week end tryst. I could almost see the smirk on their faces as they lounged in the hot tub, with a drink in hand, on Mark's dime. I listened to her until I just couldn't contain myself any longer. I stopped her short and let her know how difficult it was for me to stand by watching her throw everything away on two people who were just using her and Mark for their own selfish needs. I hoped I was getting through to her when suddenly she began to cry and tearfully replied,

"I just couldn't do it without them." She whimpered. "I owe them so much! Carla is so good to Mark and me. You have no idea." She said trying to convince me of her feelings for them.

At that point I had to resist the urge to hang up on her. Instead, I decided to try and get her to see how twisted her thinking was when it came to the two of them, so when she was finished with what she was saying I tried reasoning with her.

I calmly asked, "Didn't you hire them? Don't you pay them a wage? Don't you think that's enough? You pay them to do a job and I'm sure you pay them very well. If you don't mind me asking exactly what do they get from you?"

Answering, she said, "I pay her for helping out with Mark through his government funding each month and now because he's staying there all the time I let them have his disability check, as well and I've given Matt signing authority for it so if need be he can just go to the bank and withdraw whatever he needs for Mark every month. On top of that, if they help me out around here with the kennel I pay them a wage out of the business account. Then sometimes I give them a little treat, like a small vacation, to keep them happy and make it worth their while to stay working here. I know it sounds like a lot but it's worth it to me."

"Can't you see they're making a fortune off of you and Mark?" I exclaimed frantically trying to get her to see what they were doing. "Do you really think you can afford to pay them as much as you do? Just look at everything you hand over to them!" I stated firmly. "You're not made of money you know!"

Sarah cut in, "They help me a lot and I'm just so tired these days! I couldn't manage if it weren't for them. A lot of times I can't make it in to do shopping or go to the bank so Carla will offer to go for me. She helps me make a lot of business decisions and don't forget they help with the kennel and take care of Mark too. I just couldn't do it all myself."

I could tell I wasn't getting through to her and knowing what I knew about the entire situation, I knew I couldn't hold back any longer, so I closed my eyes, took a deep breath and dove right in.

"Sarah, I know you won't like what I have to say to you right now but I'm going to say it anyways. Matt and Carla are taking advantage of you and Mark. They are robbing you blind. I just can't believe you've agreed to pay for Carla's pardon out of Mark's trust. She was charged with theft for God's sake! She's as guilty as sin but you still continue to think she's innocent of the charges. She was convicted because she was guilty! She was using Mark to steal! He shouldn't be paying for her pardon. It's just not right how you ignore the facts about her!"

I paused to take a breath. "Then there's your drinking." I said. "Over the past couple of years your drinking has become a real problem and I think if you could get a handle on that you and Robert might be able to manage everything just fine by yourselves. You did it before those two leeches came into your life and you can do it again. I really don't believe you're capable of quitting drinking on your own at this point and you will need to find help in order to stop. I know for a fact between Matt and Carla's meddling and your excessive drinking you and Robert are experiencing serious problems in your relationship. You need to get a handle on everything real soon or you're going to lose everything you've worked so hard to achieve. And that is how I feel about everything!"

When I finished, I could hear her crying and I began to feel bad about being so abrupt, so I softly added,

"I'm only telling you this because I care about you Sarah. I can see what's happening and I'm really concerned about you."

The other end of the phone remained silent for the longest time and I hoped I'd finally gotten through to her when I heard her say,

"I know my drinking has gotten out of hand and I do plan to take care of that soon but as far as Matt and Carla go, you are wrong! They are good people with big hearts and they are there for me. I'm sorry you don't understand but I need them right now."

My heart sank knowing nothing I said made a bit of difference to her, so I continued,

"I think once you get help with your drinking you'll see things differently. I don't want you to be upset with me but I just have to let you know how I see things and how I feel about it. It's so hard for me to stand back and watch your life spiral out of control. You're a good hearted person, Sarah, with good intentions and I hate to think of anyone taking advantage of you. Just remember I'm on your side. OK? So, call me soon."

As I hung up the phone the tears flowed down my face in frustration. *What kind of hold do these people have on my sister and what is it going to take for her to see their true motives?* I thought to myself. This whole scenario weighed heavy on my heart and I was very troubled over what I could see was happening. Perplexed and confused I thought of the incredibly strong willed, self-assured, productive woman my sister had once been, just a few short years ago, compared to the weepy, down trodden, completely dependent person she had become today and I shuddered to think of what was down the road for her.

It didn't matter where I was or where I went Sarah and Mark were never far from my thoughts. It seemed the only time I had a reprieve from the turmoil going on was when Doug and I purposely took time to enjoy the many blessings surrounding us at home. It could be something as simple as sitting on the back deck in the evening that would render us totally oblivious to the cares of the outside world. Pacified by the soothing sounds of the river and mesmerized by the moon light dancing across the surface of the water we'd be transported to a special place of complete tranquility. These simple moments spent together are what made life bearable for us. Our home became our saving grace.

~ Chapter Five ~

"Only trust someone who understands these three things about you, the sorrow behind your smile, the love behind your anger and the reason behind your silence."
~ Unknown

Carla's presence continued to hover over Sarah's life like a dark cloud. The damaging influence she had on Sarah was obvious and became evident to anyone who was close to the situation by the increased isolation and dependency Sarah was now experiencing. Feeling threatened, Robert kept in touch with us more often than usual to express his grave concern about Sarah and the hopelessness he felt about the deterioration of their relationship. He claimed he was at the end of his rope and blamed the sorry state of their lives on Sarah's drinking and the ever present chaos imposed on them by Carla. We all recognized the dilemma he was facing but we stood by helpless.

This year happened to produce a bountiful harvest and although I hadn't grown a garden myself I was inundated with a large variety of freshly picked vegetables from our neighbor's garden, so I'd set aside the day for pickling and preserving the treasure trove of greens sitting on my counter. No sooner were the Mason jars set out when suddenly the phone rang. It was early in the morning, so I played with the idea of ignoring the call until I saw it was Sarah. Curious to know why she was calling at this time of day I picked up. Clearly she was quite intoxicated and very upset. Through her tears she managed to tell me the police had charged Robert with assault and taken him to jail the night before.

I was shocked, when I finally grasped what she was saying. I blurted out, "Oh my God, Sarah, what happened!?"

Continuing to sob she answered, "Honestly, I didn't think they'd take him away to jail! He's a good man. That's not what I expected to happen!"

Curious to know the details, I urged her to settle down and just tell me what had taken place.

She took a moment to quiet herself, then, began to explain. "Well, I went to visit Mark at Carla's yesterday morning and after having a few drinks I ended up staying all day. When I got home it was late and Robert was in bed. I went into the bedroom to check on him. He woke up and was really angry, yelling at me to get out. I stood there refusing to leave until he explained what was wrong, that's when he jumped out of bed. Next thing I knew he picked me up by my throat and threw me out into the hall, slamming the door on my leg. He looked like he'd been drinking all day and I was frightened, so I called the police. When they got here they looked at my bruises and spoke to both of us separately. Next thing I knew they had Robert in handcuffs and were putting him in the cruiser. The officer told me they were going to take him to the station and charge him with assault. I honestly didn't think that was going to happen! I really didn't mean to have him charged! It's just that he got physical with me and I just wanted to scare him. Oh God, what am I going to do?"

I took a moment to assess the situation before replying, "I think if the police have charged him, it's out of your hands Sarah. I don't think there's anything you can do about it. Are you going to be alright?"

"I'll be fine. I think I'm going to give Carla a call and see if I can spend a few days over there." She said.

Feeling the full impact of what was happening I realized I needed time to myself to think things over, so we talked a while longer, then I cut our conversation short. "Listen Sarah, I have to go. I'll call you later today, OK? Just hang in there!"

As I hung up the phone I was feeling a little guilty about ending our talk. I knew she needed me right now and I should be there for her but I was finding it more and more difficult to speak to her when she was drinking and quite frankly, I was getting tired of having to deal with the constant drama in her life. I even thought about distancing myself from her and her problems but as much as I tried to get her out of my mind I just couldn't turn my back on her. I returned to the chore of canning but my mind remained distracted with our conversation. Later that afternoon I gave in to my better judgment and called her back knowing full well I'd be pulled right back into the thick of things.

The weeks that followed were clearly the beginning of the end of their relationship. Robert couldn't get over the fact Sarah had called the police on him and turned resentful towards her. Sarah on the other hand, knew how upset Robert was and was afraid of what he might do if he were allowed to go near her. The police kept Robert in jail over the weekend until a bail hearing could be arranged. Meantime, to protect herself, Sarah applied for a restraining order to keep Robert from coming around her. The order stated he stay away from her and the house as long as she was living there, even though it was his house she was living in. This caused even more resentment on Robert's part and the situation continued to escalate day by day.

A trial date, to deal with the assault charges, was set for the spring. Sarah hired herself a lawyer and began preparing the case against Robert. It was no surprise to me when I learned Carla was attending every single lawyer's appointment with her. In fact, Carla placed herself right in the middle of this whole issue between Sarah and Robert, advising and consoling Sarah throughout the entire time. For Sarah's sake, I was glad to know she had someone close by to help her through this difficult time but on the other hand I had the feeling Carla was pleased to see Robert out of the picture and would not be in favor of them reconciling, leaving me to question the advice she was giving Sarah. From what Sarah told me, Carla was egging her on to get rid of Robert because she didn't think Sarah needed him around anymore, referring to Robert as a leech and a loser. The unfortunate thing about that is that Sarah was put in the awkward position of having to choose between the man she loved and a woman she felt indebted to.

By now Mark was well established in his trailer at Carla's place. I was surprised when he called one day to ask if Doug and I would like to attend a housewarming party he was planning to hold in early November. Now that Mark was living in his trailer full time he was excited to show it off to his family and friends. Naturally we accepted the invitation and told him we'd be there. A few weeks later we packed up and made the long trip east to Sarah's for Mark's party. When we pulled out of the driveway it was the perfect day for a road trip but as the day progressed the weather started to turn nasty. Snow and freezing rain made the roads hazardous. We considered turning back but when we thought of how disappointed Mark would have been if we didn't show up we continued on. Finally pulling up to the trailer and seeing Mark waiting at the door to greet us we were glad we'd made the decision to continue on, regardless of the weather conditions.

Mark proved to be a wonderful host as he took our coats and offered us drinks and food after our seemingly endless, nerve-wracking drive. Soon Sarah appeared and was glad to see we'd made the trip safe and sound. Once inside we noticed Matt and Carla sitting off to the side. As usual Carla was hiding behind her sunglasses, appearing detached from all the activity. On the other hand Mark was right in his element as he greeted everyone and made sure they were comfortable. A steady stream of people filtered in and out of the trailer all evening long. We watched Mark as he delighted in mingling with his guests. It was amusing to see the glow on his face and the pride he had in showing off his new home to everyone who was interested in taking his tour. Anticipating this night for a long time and now that it had finally arrived Mark reveled in being the life of the party.

After our tour of the trailer we were left with a number of concerns, so we went in search of Matt to see if he could answer our questions. Once we caught up with him he began by answering to us about the heating. Apparently, it was heated by propane but because the tanker truck couldn't reach the back of the property to fill up the large tank behind the trailer Matt was forced to refill small BBQ tanks purchased at the local Canadian Tire store daily to heat the space.

He went on to say, "The one drawback with that is they aren't very efficient and they have to be replaced every day and that's a pain but what are you going to do?"

Doug and I rolled our eyes and shook our heads at the thought of a trailer this size being heated with BBQ tanks. What if the tanks ran out of fuel before Matt refilled them? Voicing our concern Matt reassured us he replaced them each day in plenty of time.

When we first arrived we'd noticed an extension cord running under the trailer so we asked Matt what it was used for. He told us the municipality had a bylaw that wouldn't allow a second residence on their property so they decided to wait before hooking up any utilities permanently. The extension cord was hooked up to the main house and the cord ran about two hundred feet along the snow covered ground to the electrical panel in the trailer. We suspected the panel was overloaded and that was the reason for the fuses blowing all night long. It didn't appear very safe but Matt reassured us he would have it hooked up properly as soon as he could.

Later that evening Mark pointed out to us that he had to put a plastic bag over the toilet seat and throw it out after he was finished going to the bathroom because there was no plumbing hooked up. When we approached Matt about the situation regarding the plumbing he told us it was another job on his to do list once they were sure the municipality was going to allow the trailer to be parked there.

Matt chuckled when he finished with his explanations, "Oh well, it's just Mark living out here and as long as he's got his TV to watch and a cold can of coke to drink, nothing else matters to him and he's happy."

Left trying to digest the condescending remarks Matt directed toward Mark and the flimsy explanations he gave for the state of the trailer I found it necessary to go outside for a breath of fresh air. While standing on the step I noticed quite a bit of snow had fallen since we arrived and wondered who was responsible for shoveling a path so Mark could get back and forth to the house. Just then Matt passed by, so I took the opportunity to ask him who shovels the snow?

He answered sarcastically, "Shovel? Oh no, we don't have to worry about shoveling. We just wait until Mark beats a path to our door." Then before we had a chance to discuss anything more with him, he was off.

Listening to his smug answers and seeing for ourselves the living conditions Mark was expected to live in we knew we had to have a discussion with Sarah but tonight was not the time or place.

It was a great party but unfortunately the icy road conditions made it necessary for us to leave early. On the trip home, I couldn't get the conditions Mark was expected to live in out of my mind.

I was left with so many questions. *What happens if Matt was late in hooking the tank up? Would Mark know enough to go to the main house for heat? What if he was sleeping when the heat went off? Could he freeze to death? The set up with the electrical didn't seem safe either. What if there was a fire? Would Mark be able to get out*? The questions were endless and I wondered why Mark was expected to live without the plumbing being hooked up, not to mention, him having to trudge through the snow instead of making sure a path was shoveled for him or, at least, give him a shovel so he could shovel it himself. It all seemed so indignant and disrespectful.

After a very restless night, I called Sarah to try and get some answers to my questions about what was going on with the trailer and point out my disgust at the make shift conditions Mark was living in.

When she picked up I started by telling her, "You know, Sarah, that trailer may have been sufficient for him to live in during the warmer weather but pretty soon we'll be right in the thick of winter with sub zero temperatures. What happens then?"

Trying to ease my mind, she answered, "Don't worry. Matt and Carla have full intentions of getting him a proper heat source and hooking him up with plumbing and a proper electrical system, once they're sure the municipality isn't going to make them remove the trailer.

I cut in, "I don't get it, Sarah. How could you put Mark in this position? What really irritates me is how they're so condescending towards him. Mark can't speak up for himself and it's as though his comfort and safety doesn't matter. It's like they're continually making fun of him. It's just not right!"

"That's just the way they are, always joking around. They don't mean any harm. Do you think maybe you're being a little touchy about things?" She asked, trying to minimize my concerns.

"No, I don't!"I firmly answered.

When we hung up, I thought over what Sarah had said then thought to myself. *Maybe it is me. Maybe I am too harsh on them and overly protective of Mark.* At that point I began to recall all the reasons I had such distrust for these people and why I doubted Sarah's judgment in the first place. Suddenly, I felt vindicated in bringing my concerns about Mark's living conditions up to Sarah but in the end I had to accept the fact I could only tell her what I thought when it came to Mark. She was his guardian and ultimately, the final say was hers and now with Matt and Carla in the mix my opinion didn't stand a chance. Short of causing a major rift between Sarah and me by calling the authorities and the possibility of everything resulting in a court case, there was nothing I could do about the situation. It was out of my hands.

A few days later in mid-afternoon Sarah called and I could tell by the sound of her voice she had been drinking quite heavily.

"Are you busy right now?" she asked. "I want to talk to you about something."

"Nope, I'm not doing a thing right now" I answered. "Sounds serious, what is it?"

"Well," she began, "I just wanted to tell you I'm thinking of changing my will. I don't see any reason to keep Robert on as executor seeing as our relationship is coming to an end. I'm thinking of appointing Carla in his place. I was going to ask you to be the executor but Carla is familiar with my business dealings, as well as all my personal affairs so it just makes sense to have things set up that way. Besides, she lives in this area, so it will just be easier for her to deal with matters. I'm going to arrange it so my estate will be divided equally between Carla, Mark and you and I've already made the three of you equal beneficiaries of my life insurance. Oh, and by the way." She added, "Carla has arranged to have the will drawn up by a lawyer friend of hers here in town. He says he'll give me a deal. What do you think?"

I felt very uneasy listening to her talk about such a sensitive topic. Eventually, I told her as long as she felt comfortable with the way she was thinking of arranging her will then she should go ahead with it. After hanging up I sat trying to convince myself there was nothing to worry about Sarah's intentions to appoint Carla as the executor of her will. The only experience I'd had with being an executor of someone's will was after mom passed away when Sarah and I were appointed co- executors. *What harm could come of Carla being Sarah's executor?* I asked myself. *It's all legal and pretty straight forward. You just carry out the person's wishes, step by step, exactly as the will states. Mom's will was very explicit and from what Sarah told me the original will she'd had drawn up, appointing Robert as executor, was quite detailed too. Sarah had always been very precise about her affairs, so I'm positive she'll make sure everything is drawn up properly.*" Convinced there was nothing to be concerned about I laid the matter to rest.

A few weeks passed when early one morning I answered the phone and could hear Sarah sobbing on the other end. It was difficult to understand what she was saying but eventually she calmed down enough for me to be able to make her words out. Apparently, she had received a letter from Robert's lawyer telling her she had one month to vacate the premises. "Robert wants his house back!" She ranted.

"How could he do this to me?" she wailed. "He knows I have nowhere to go with all these dogs. What am I going to do? I've spent most of my money fixing this place up! Where will I go?"

I quickly cut her off, "Settle down Sarah. There's no sense in getting yourself all upset. That won't do anyone any good. My guess is that in the eyes of the law you are a tenant living in his house and he may have the right to evict you. I think you need to go see a lawyer to see what rights you have and if there's anything you can do about it. I'm sure he can't throw you out just like that. Be sure to make an appointment today, OK?"

We continued to talk until Sarah agreed to call a lawyer and before hanging up she promised to let me know as soon as she had any news.

When Sarah got home after seeing the lawyer she called me. As I picked up I recognized the familiar sounds of ice cubes tinkling in the background. When I asked if she'd been drinking she ignored my question, so I reiterated, "I hope you're not driving when you drink."

"No, Carla always does the driving if I've had a drink. I wouldn't be that stupid." She answered. "Anyways, I just got home from talking to the lawyer and apparently there is something I can do to stay in this house but it means taking Robert to court again."

"Really? Then it is a good thing you did check with a lawyer after all." I said.

She continued, "The lawyer says there's something in the law called 'Undo Enrichment'. He thinks I can file a claim against Robert because when we moved in here after the renters moved out it was in pretty rough shape and because I used my money to cover the costs of all the remodeling and improvements done around here, the value of the property has almost doubled. Robert can do one of two things. He can either pay me the difference of what the property is worth now as opposed to what it was worth before I put my money into it or he can let me buy him out. The best part is I don't have to leave here until everything is settled in the courts and the restraining order stays in effect until that time."

"Well, that's a relief. I'm really happy for you." I said as I let out a sigh.

I really was sincere about being happy for her but a little piece of me felt badly for Robert. I liked him from the first time I met him. I also understood how devastated he must be after all he's been put through over the past few years but when push came to shove I had to stand behind my sister.

For Sarah the following months were a constant stream of lawyer's appointments, affidavits, and he said, she said accusations. Of course, Carla was staying close by and attending all appointments at the lawyers with her. As much as I was pleased to know Sarah had someone close by to support her through this complicated ordeal, I couldn't help but question Carla's intentions and her influence on Sarah's decisions. At some point I gave up trying to keep up with everything that was going on with the courts because I was more concerned with how Sarah's physical and mental health was deteriorating. She'd lost a tremendous amount of weight and from what she told me she had no appetite for food at all, although, it was obvious she hadn't lost her hunger for booze. She began taking pills to help her get to sleep and pills to perk her up. She felt her life and livelihood depended on whether she was able to remain in the house or was forced to leave. She became totally obsessed with winning this court case and the stress and strain was taking a toll on her.

It was becoming difficult for Sarah to hide her depression. When I spoke to her she was either crying when I called or would start crying, before we finished our conversation. We would talk endlessly as I tried to convince her to get help for her drinking. I was trying to make her see if she'd stop drinking she would feel so much better about herself but my words fell on deaf ears. It was frustrating because I knew if she did give up drinking she'd be able to start dealing with her problems on her own instead of having to lean on others for help and maybe if she started seeing things clearly she might realize things aren't as bad as they appear to her. It didn't matter what I said she was in total denial about her addiction to alcohol and ignored my advice. It was very sad to watch as she became more and more fragile both mentally and physically. At one point, I even told her she should walk away from it all and start fresh because it just wasn't worth what she was doing to herself. It was tearing me apart inside to watch her waste away before my very eyes. I didn't know what to do for her except to be there if she needed me and to pray for her recovery to health.

One day in early summer while we were visiting for the weekend I was surprised to hear Sarah say she was starting into counseling. *Finally, an answer to my prayers, she's ready to get help for herself.* I thought with a smile.

"That's great, Sarah! When do you start?"

"I begin this week! Can you imagine I got right in to see them. I guess it's about time I start to deal with my drinking. Actually, I'm really looking forward to being able to think straight again." She admitted.

Sarah sounded determined about her decision to get counseling for her drinking and I immediately detected a positive note in her outlook on life but her turnaround was very short lived. Within a few weeks I could hear the old Sarah start to creep back in again. In the beginning, she was optimistic and looking forward to the future but soon I began noticing subtle changes in her. She sounded as though she was carrying the troubles of the world on her shoulders. No doubt, when I stopped to look at everything she was dealing with I could see why she felt so overwhelmed. The uncertainty of not knowing if she would have a roof over her head or if she would be able to continue running the kennel must have been agonizing for her. Not to mention the breakdown of her relationship with Robert and the unrest of the assault charge. She must have felt helpless, her life and livelihood were out of her control. Her future lay in the hands of the courts.

So it didn't surprise me when Sarah called and once again I heard the all too familiar tinkle of ice cubes and the slurring of her words when she began talking.

"I just can't do it anymore. It's just too hard." She said, sounding feeble and weak.

"Of course you can, Sarah. Given the alternative, you have no choice but to do it", I said, trying to lighten her mood.

"Seriously, I don't want to continue on. I'm just so tired. I just want to end it all." She sighed.

"Oh Sarah, please don't talk like that." I pleaded as I began to realize she really meant what she was saying.

"I can't help it, that's how I feel. It's just too hard for me to continue on. I want out and I've been thinking of ways to do it. It would have to be quick and it would definitely have to do the job once and for all." She said matter of factly, as if she was talking about the weather.

"What? What are you saying, Sarah? What brought all this on?" I questioned in disbelief of what I was hearing.

Her words were chilling, making the hair on the back of my neck stand up as my mind frantically searched for the right words to say to her. She had obviously given this a lot of thought and I was caught off guard. It took a few minutes for the true meaning of her disturbing words to sink in before I continued,

"I hope you realize, Sarah, suicide is a permanent solution to a temporary problem."

I was trying my best to console her and that was the only thing I could think of saying to her, hoping she would grasp the truth that lay in that one significant statement. We stayed connected and talked for a very long time after that but I had no way of knowing how she perceived my urging and hoped something I said would help her to see how twisted her thinking was. Deep down I knew she was far too self-absorbed with everything going on in her life right now to listen to reason and my heart broke for her. It was very difficult ending our conversation that day and I remember making a point of not saying goodbye to her so we both parted by agreeing to "talk again soon."

After hanging up I didn't know how to react to what my sister just told me. *After all, what could I do to help her? I'm four hours away, so what could I possibly do to help?* I kept repeating these thoughts over and over in my head while I digested the content of our conversation. I tried to get on with my day but I was haunted by Sarah's misery. Five agonizing minutes later, I picked up the phone and called the police in Sarah's area. I couldn't get out fast enough what had transpired between Sarah and me. When I felt they had enough information to understand the urgency of my call I asked if there was anything they could do to help her. They asked for her address assuring me I had done the right thing and said they would send someone out to see her right away.

Knowing Sarah was all alone I had no choice but to contact Carla to alert her. I told her I had just called the police and they were heading to Sarah's right now. I asked if she would go there just to be with her. We talked for a few minutes regarding Sarah's condition and we both agreed it was time she got professional help. Carla agreed to go to Sarah's right away to be there to support her. I knew Sarah would be upset with me for calling the police and probably wouldn't want to speak with me, so I asked Carla to call me later to let me know what happened.

It was several hours later when I finally heard back from Carla. She explained it took the police a long time to talk Sarah into going to the hospital and even though the ambulance was waiting to take her she insisted Carla drive her there. After checking in at the hospital she made sure Sarah was settled into a room and resting before she left. We had a very lengthy conversation that night and in the end we both agreed Sarah was in the right place to get the help she so desperately needed. Carla also noted that Sarah was very upset with me and didn't want to have anything to do with me right now. I wasn't surprised to hear her say that Sarah didn't want to speak to me but when she told me I had to go through her now to speak to Sarah or Mark I was taken aback and realized I'd been put in a position I'd hoped I'd never have to be in, dependent on Carla. Regardless, my main focus right then was Sarah's well-being not Carla's ego, so, I just had to accept that's the way things were, for now.

Early the following day I called Carla to see if she'd spoken to Sarah that morning and find out how she was doing.

"She's home." Carla answered nonchalantly.

"What?" I shrieked, unable to believe what I was hearing.

Then, she repeated, "She's home. After I got home last night Sarah called and wanted me to come and get her. So I drove back to the hospital and brought her back home. She was home by one o'clock. She even asked if I'd bring a bottle with me so she could have a drink on the way. She really sounded like she could use a good shot."

"Are you kidding me? You mean to tell me you picked her up, supplied her with a bottle and drove her home? I thought we both agreed she needs help!" I screamed into the phone.

Carla quickly cut me off. "Let me explain something to you. Sarah is my employer. I am her employee. If she asks me to discharge her from the hospital, I discharge her from the hospital. If she wants me to bring her booze, I bring her booze. That's just the way it is and besides it won't do any good to get her help with her drinking until everything with the house and Robert are settled in the courts."

I certainly didn't see it that way and once again my suspicions were aroused. Her answer caused me to question her intentions and left me feeling disheartened by the fact that she now had complete control of my sister and my brother and I was left with no other choice but to cow tow to her if I wanted to keep in touch with them. Sarah was going through some very difficult times right now and it upset me not to be able to be there for her. Not to mention having to rely on Carla for my contact with Mark too. I knew I had to keep my cool with Carla while keeping my guard up knowing what she was capable of.

In the midst of being detached from Sarah, the day finally arrived for the assault case against Robert to be heard in court and I was left waiting anxiously for Carla's email to let me know the outcome. While I sat there I thought of how quickly Sarah and Robert's relationship had deteriorated and what a bitter sweet day this was for me. With great anticipation, I opened Carla's email to find Robert had been found guilty as charged. I was conflicted. I didn't know if I should laugh or cry, whether I should be happy for Sarah or sad for Robert. I called Carla to see how Sarah was taking Robert's conviction. Carla told me Sarah was as good as to be expected and was lying down right then. Once again I tried to get Carla to see the urgency of Sarah receiving help for her drinking and the depression she was experiencing. Carla was adamant about her getting no benefit from help, of any kind, until all the court hearings were over. Carla made it clear she was in complete control and I was forced to drop the subject. Then to add insult to injury, she warned me not to bother trying to contact Sarah at all because of how upset she was with me. I agreed not to call her because I knew it was just a matter of time before she would come around and realize I never meant her any harm by calling the police and until that time Carla was something I just had to resign myself to put up with.

I hung up feeling bewildered, defeated and helpless. It was beyond me how Carla didn't see the necessity of getting help for Sarah. She had witnessed Sarah's extensive drinking and she was well aware of her deep depression and didn't seem to care. I realized how fragile Sarah's mental state was and I wasn't sure how much longer she could go on like this. The hearing regarding the house wasn't going to be heard until the fall and I just prayed Sarah would make it till then.

~ Chapter Six ~

"Rock bottom is the foundation
on which I rebuilt my life."
~J.K. Rowling

Even though Sarah was refusing to speak to me I knew, that given time, she would get over being upset. What really bothered me was how vulnerable her and Mark were and the fact they were both left to the mercy of a woman who was a proven liar and a thief, who seemed to get some sort of sick satisfaction out of controlling my siblings. Regardless of my opinion of Carla I found myself in the position of having to rely on her word to keep me informed of how they were doing. The deceitful behavior I'd witnessed in the past caused me great concern in leaving her in control. Although Carla would contact me by email and phone, from time to time, to keep me up to date on what was happening with Sarah and Mark, I really didn't know what to believe about anything she said. Were they really fine? Were they doing as well as could be expected? Mine and Carla's outlook on life was as different as night and day, making it hard for me to know for sure how things actually were.

Mark was living full time at Carla's now, and apparently from what she told me Sarah's drinking was nonstop from morning till night. She said Sarah was constantly calling her demanding to see Mark and showing up at all times of the day and night wanting to visit with him. She let me know her patience with Sarah was wearing thin and she didn't know what she was going to do with her. I listened to Carla's complaints but I had no idea of what to tell her, after all, there was nothing I could do as long as Sarah wasn't speaking to me. I was left to patiently wait for her to contact me. The only advice I could give was to suggest we try to get Sarah the help she so desperately needed but Carla continued to insist it would do no good to try and deal with Sarah's drinking until everything in the courts had been taken care of. I didn't understand her reasoning and let her know how strongly I disagreed with her. The fact was I was left at the mercy of Carla's word, until one day in mid-summer the phone rang.

"Hi Robin, how're you doing?"

I couldn't believe my own ears, it was Sarah! I was never so glad to hear someone's voice as I was to hear hers on the other end of the phone that day.

"I think the question is how are you doing? It's so good to hear from you, Sarah." I cried out.

"I want to apologize to you Robin. I know you were only trying to help me. I hope you'll forgive me, I was so messed up." She earnestly admitted.

"That's OK. I understand." I said, thankful she was finally speaking to me.

"I'm back into counseling at the hospital now and I'm feeling much better about things. I go there during the week and come home on weekends". She explained.

"Wonderful! I'm really happy to hear that Sarah. How's Mark doing?"

"As far as I know he's fine but there's something I need to get your opinion on."

"What's that Sarah?'"

"Well, in the spring, after Carla got her pardon and she went away to Arizona for two weeks, she left Jennifer, her sixteen year old daughter, in charge of Mark while she was gone. I offered to take him while she was away but she insisted he be left with Jennifer. While she was away I went there to have a visit with him and was told her mom had left strict orders; I was not allowed to see him or go near him while she was away. She's only sixteen years old and she's not very responsible. I just can't believe Carla would leave Mark with her and not even allow me to see him. What do you think of that?"

"I don't know what to say about that Sarah. It doesn't sound right to me that she can keep you away from your own brother but I wasn't involved at that time so I don't know all the circumstances."

"That's OK. I just thought it was kind of strange and wanted to run it past you."

"Does she let you see him now?" I asked.

"Only if she's there but she doesn't allow him to come home and stay with me anymore. She keeps him right under her wing."

"Well, that's troubling. Let me give it some thought and I'll get back to you." I told her.

After we hung up I did give serious thought to the conversation we just had. Even though I didn't trust Carla I could understand her not allowing Mark to stay alone with Sarah or letting him go home alone with her because of her drinking. On the other hand, if Sarah had truly given up drinking then there's no reason why she shouldn't be able to see Mark. It was a difficult situation to have an opinion on since I'd been alienated from their lives for so long. While thinking things over, it occurred to me that Carla was in the perfect position to have complete control over Mark and if she chose to do so she could keep both of us from having any kind of contact with him at all. I felt sick at heart just thinking about the possibility and prayed it would never come to that. Ultimately, I had no clout when it came to decisions regarding Mark and there was very little I could do to change anything. If anything was to be decided on, regarding Mark, Sarah was the one who had to take a stand with Carla.

Sarah and I were enjoying our reunion and kept close contact with each other after that. Carla began to loosen the tight hold she had on Mark and everything seemed to be running smoothly for a time.

It was one of those hot sultry days in late July when Sarah called me in the afternoon. She was so excited I could hardly make out what she was trying to get across to me. After asking her to slow down I was eventually able to understand what she was saying. She explained a TV show called "Puppy Luv" had contacted her to see if she would like to be featured in one of their episodes. They said her kennel had been suggested as a contender and they would like to arrange an interview with her and her Maltese puppies.

"I just can't believe it!" She kept saying, over and over again. "Do you know what an impact this will have on the kennel? I'm so glad the work on the house is finished, just in case, they need to film inside but I just don't know how I'll handle being interviewed! This is great! Can you imagine the exposure? Me and my precious little puppies on TV! Wow, I just can't believe it!"

I smiled to myself. It sounded as though things were finally starting to turn in her favor. She was even starting to visit Mark at his trailer now and sometimes spent the night there with him. She told me he loved playing host and was very attentive to her. Always asking if she was comfortable and constantly making sure she had something to eat. We both laughed and thought it was cute that the meals he offered her consisted of chocolate chip cookies, pudding cups and a can of diet coke. Before hanging up she said she would give me a call after the interview to let me know how everything went. I continued to smile long after our conversation ended knowing things were finally going well for her.

While I waited for Sarah to call on the day of the interview, I hoped everything was still going well. When the phone finally rang she told me they were set to start filming sometime in August and the show would be aired on October 31. I let out a sigh of relief. Over the next few weeks Sarah was kept busy getting the house in order for the taping and talked about nothing else. She was trying to make room for the cameras in her tiny living room and even went out and purchased a new leather couch and a new outfit. She wanted everything to be just perfect for the day of filming. The gardens had to be manicured and there was a little bit of painting that still had to be completed after the renovation but most importantly the dogs and puppies had to be groomed to perfection. After working non-stop from morning till night things were finally ready for the filming crew to arrive the following day, Sarah was ecstatic, albeit stressed to the max. At the end of the day she couldn't wait to tell me how everything went.

"You won't believe it! What a day! They came in here and rearranged all the furniture so they could get the right angles when they were shooting. Half of the living room furniture was taken right out but thankfully they left the new couch where it was so I was glad of that. They gave me a script to memorize and I don't know how I did it but I think I did OK. There were a couple of times we had to do a part over but I think it went pretty well overall. It was just so hot in the house between the weather and all the lights, they had to keep stopping to redo my makeup and I just can't believe how everything was so staged and scripted but it was good. It was really good! What an experience!"

"So, I guess you think you're a celebrity now, do you? I kidded.

"Well, not exactly but I sure hope it helps with getting the kennel on the map." She replied.

"So you won't tell me how the story ends, eh? I questioned

"Nope, I'm going to keep you guessing. You have to watch the show to find out if one of my puppies were picked. It's going to air on October 31, so make sure you watch it."

"I wouldn't miss it for the world, Sarah."

As we ended our conversation I sensed Sarah was on cloud nine and she was savoring every minute of it.

The next time we talked Sarah was very excited to hear from me. Apparently, she'd been busy planning a "New Beginnings" party for the middle of October and wanted to invite Doug and me. She figured everything would be finished with her court case by then and regardless of whether she was able to remain in the house or not, she was prepared to begin her new life. She was still feeling regret about her relationship with Robert having to end this way, but she had come to accept they had both lost the love and respect they once felt for each other and there was no choice but to go their separate ways. She was ready to move on and was looking forward to the next chapter in her life. Listening to her optimism that day was like music to my ears.

Sarah's enthusiasm continued as plans for her party progressed and more importantly she was sounding like her old self again. Anxious to show off the results of her newly renovated house she talked about getting in touch with a few of her old friends from her previous job that she hadn't seen for years. She loved to play hostess and thought inviting them for lunch would be a great way for her to reunite with them and bring them back into her life again.

The day of the luncheon I waited until I was sure everyone had left before I called to see how things turned out. It was hard for Sarah to contain herself as she relayed the highlights of the day to me. Apparently, everyone raved about the meal she prepared for them and from experience I knew she would have gone all out to please her guests. I can only imagine the feast that would have been set out for them. Happy to meet up with each other again the day was spent rehashing old times and catching up on each other's lives. They met each other years ago while working together and because they were familiar with Mark much of the conversation centered on him. They were all interested in hearing how he was doing.

September came around and the greatly anticipated day of court finally arrived. Sarah's future depended on the outcome of this hearing, so waiting to hear the verdict was almost unbearable for us. I know she said she was ready to get on with her life regardless of how the hearing turned out but I know it would have been a crushing blow for her if she lost the case. Her whole world would have turned upside down and I feared what might happen with her if she lost the house. My thoughts were focused on Sarah from the time I got up that morning until I finally received word from her in late afternoon. When the phone rang I knew it was her. *Dear God, please let it be good news* I thought before picking up. Then, I heard her joyful cry,

"I got it Robin! I got the house! Robert agreed if I buy him out he will sign the house over to me. Oh, I'm so happy! All I have to do now is send the papers over to his lawyer to have Robert sign them."

"That's wonderful Sarah, I'm so glad to hear everything turned out so well." I answered, feeling relieved it was finally over.

Obtaining the house was a huge milestone in Sarah's life. It meant being able to continue with running the kennel. Without the kennel she would have no source of income and for a woman who was just about to turn fifty-nine that was a big deal. She had every right to fear losing the property and every right to celebrate being able to remain there. Now she could begin making definite plans for her future. It was during this conversation Sarah informed me she was planning to apply to Children's Aid to become a foster parent. She felt she had a lot to offer and would enjoy fostering a couple of young teen girls.

Now that she was sole owner of the house she talked about remodeling the garage into a large bedroom with a washroom and a huge closet and felt that would give enough room to comfortably house two girls.

"Of course, this means I'd have to quickly build a kennel out back for the puppies." She said enthusiastically.

It was refreshing listening to her make plans for her future. She was beginning to look at all the possibilities open to her, possibilities she wasn't able to even comprehend a few months earlier. I was so proud of her.

The "New Beginnings" party Sarah was planning was only one week away. She arranged for Matt to do all the cooking on the grill which would leave her free to be hostess. As soon as we arrived that evening she took us on a quick tour of the house pointing out all the changes that were done during the renovation. Sarah had always had a flair for decorating and it was truly amazing what she'd done with the place. It was so chic, so Sarah. The house quickly filled with her friends and I was so glad to see Mark when he showed up with Carla. The ambiance was joyful and an extravagant feast of lobster, chicken, steak and all the fixings was offered for our eating pleasure. All this coupled with a never ending supply of fine wine ensured that the evening turned out to be a fabulous success!

It was a great party and we would have loved to take Sarah up on her offer to stay over but unfortunately Doug had promised to do a job for someone the following morning, making it impossible for us to spend the night. When it was time for us to leave Sarah and Mark followed us outside to say good-bye. Standing there wishing we could stay longer we thanked Sarah for having us and apologized for not being able to stay the night. Then, after all the hugs and kisses and repeated goodbyes, we pulled out of the driveway. I watched and waved until they finally faded out of sight.

One evening, the following week I received a call from Sarah. She seemed a little edgy as she told me there were a couple of things she wanted to run past me just to get my thoughts on them.

"Sure Sarah, what is it?" I answered wondering what this was all about.

"I have some concerns about Carla. I just want to hear what you think." She said hesitantly and then began, "When Carla's son Tony, got married I lent him five thousand dollars for a down payment on a house. He was supposed to have paid it back by now but when I asked Carla about it, she said he had no intentions of paying it back because it was given as a gift."

"And was it?" I asked

"No, it was definitely a loan." She quickly answered. "The other thing is, when I go to the lawyers Carla goes with me and lately she's been taking over and answering the lawyer on my behalf. Sometimes she says things I don't agree with but she's very pushy and I don't know what to do about it". She hesitated for a moment and then added, "And I'm pretty sure the two of them have been messing with my finances."

I felt relieved Sarah was finally seeing through them and took the opportunity to tell her what I thought. "Well, for starters you need to start taking back control of your life Sarah! You have allowed the two of them to walk right over you! If it was me, I would have fired them long ago! You need to get rid of them!" I blurted out.

She simply agreed by answering, "I know." And then she added, "I plan to bring Mark back home too."

This was the very first time in eight years Sarah had ever said one word against Carla or Matt and I was so relieved to hear she was finally starting to see through them and their capers. I had always known they were up to no good and after what I'd just heard it was becoming crystal clear to me exactly what that was.

Just then Sarah broke into my thoughts and asked, "Is Doug there? Can I speak to him?"

"Sure I'll get him for you."

Doug took over the phone and suddenly I saw the look of concern wash over his face. Then I heard him ask, "Do you have any idea who it could be?" After a brief conversation he hung up and explained to me that Sarah was concerned about someone following close behind her in a car with their high beams on forcing her to speed up when she was driving at night. She asked Doug if he knew if there was anything she could do about it. He told her she should try and get the license plate number next time it happened and short of reporting the incidents to the police and staying off the roads at night there wasn't much else she could do. I was enjoying watching Sarah get on with her life and thought worrying about her was a thing of the past but after this phone call my concern for her was rekindled.

I called her a few days later to see how she was doing. She sounded great and sounded genuinely excited about her new lease on life. I was interested in knowing how everything stood with Robert signing the papers. She explained all the dates were set and things were ready to be settled. I was so happy to see the change in her. Just before we hung up Sarah asked in a rather playful manner,

"Guess what, Robin?"

"What?"

"I won!" She shouted, then without another word she hung up.

With a smile on my face and shaking my head at her wit, I hung up the phone and immediately thought to myself *but at what cost Sarah, what cost?*

Little did I know, at the time, those words would be the last words I would ever hear Sarah speak. Two weeks later, just before nine on the evening of October 31, my sister would be killed in a single car accident not far from Hampton on County Rd. 21.

~ Chapter Seven ~

"Trust is such a diverse word, it either makes something or it destroys it."
~ Anonymous

Waves of despair continued to wash over me as I went through the motions of planning Sarah's memorial. Sarah was not a Christian, so a formal service held in a funeral home, with all the usual protocol would not be appropriate for her. I wanted to offer her something special, something that would bring honor and meaning to her memory. Once I learned there was such a person as a 'Celebrant'; someone who is nondenominational and would work with the family to put together a personalized service, I called Carla to let her know of my latest discovery to see what she thought of the idea. I was glad to hear her say she thought this was something Sarah would have approved of.

Through the days of my deepest grief I consulted with Carla and together we created a day we felt Sarah would have been proud of. For whatever the reason, Carla insisted November 26 be the day set aside for the memorial and said she wanted to do the eulogy, adding, she wanted to put together a power point presentation, a tribute to Sarah's life. A close friend of Carla's and acquaintance of Sarah's, who lived nearby, offered her home to hold the service and because Sarah was killed along the side of the highway, I felt there should be a roadside ceremony as well, so I offered to put something together to be held after the service at the scene of the accident. To honor Sarah, Doug crafted a cross to be placed at the roadside to mark the location where Sarah's life ended. Word of the memorial was sent out, a simple wooden urn to hold her ashes was purchased, songs were chosen, candles were bought and food and flowers were arranged for.

While dealing with all the preparations I was simply going through the motions. I was finding it difficult to imagine life without my little sister and I found it necessary to fight back my tears while sorting through the personal belongings we brought home with us from Sarah's, in order to pick out some pictures to display at the memorial. While wrestling with my emotions a friend of mine called to tell me about an article she'd seen posted on the internet. Apparently Carla had been interviewed about Sarah's accident. After we hung up, I hesitated, undecided if I wanted to delve into the details of Sarah's demise so soon after her death but against my better judgment I went to my computer and pulled up the article titled, 'Friend Mourns Loss of Hampton Woman'.

Once I finished reading the article, an intense wave of grief came over me, bringing me into an even deeper level of anguish. As the words began to sink in, it occurred to me, this must have been what Carla was doing in the office when we were at Sarah's collecting her things. That's probably why she got so angry when Mark barged in on her. I recalled her saying something about a reporter contacting her that day but she didn't elaborate on the call. Then reading the article over a second time, I figured there must have been a misprint when it stated Mark had lived with Carla for ten years. She had only known him for eight and he'd only been living there permanently just over a year. The rest of the article focused on what a good friend Carla was to Sarah and mentioned little of Sarah's family. Knowing Carla's inflated ego like I did it was no surprise to see how far she went in stretching the truth to make it all about her. It bothered me to see her disregard us in the article but I had enough to concern myself with without trying to keep up with what Carla was up to.

After word of Sarah's death was announced our days were filled with friends dropping in to give their condolences, while the phone rang constantly with a steady stream of people giving their condolences. It was so uplifting to have people who genuinely cared surrounding us and sharing in our grief. Having people around allowed me to come out of myself and if only for a moment, it was a refreshing break from the seemingly endless sense of loss I was feeling. But at the end of the day when the door closed on the final visitor, the silence was deafening. Left to my own thoughts and feelings, I would plunge right back into the depths of despair. I couldn't help but ask why this had to happen? She had made such a turn around and gained back her zest for life. She had just reclaimed her purpose for living and now she would never get to fulfill her dreams. Beginning to fully comprehend the unfairness of it all, I was forced to come to the realization that I would never hear her voice again, never see her smile and never be able to give her a hug, ever! Life for me had forever changed but life continued on, albeit without her.

On November 8, one week after Sarah's death, I sat down to open my emails and saw there was a message from Carla. Apparently she was in Cambridge applying for Sarah's life insurance and was requesting my Social Insurance Number and permission from me to allow her to sign my name to the insurance documents so she could finish filling out the forms. She requested this be done as soon as possible because she didn't know what expenses she would face while settling the estate.

I located my S.I.N. and emailed it to her but I hesitated to give permission for her to sign my name. Knowing her past track record I didn't feel comfortable allowing her to sign anything for me without me reading it first, so I decided to call her to discuss this with her. When I finally got through to her she was still in the office at the insurance company. I told her I would like to see exactly what it was I was signing before I released my permission for her to sign and asked her to send the forms to me. That week I waited to receive the insurance papers when on the morning of November 10, I received an unexpected call from Carla.

Excitedly she began, "I just picked up mine and Mark's check from the insurance. Yours is in the mail and guess what? I thought Sarah was only insured for one hundred thousand dollars but it turns out she was insured for closer to one hundred and fifty thousand! That means we each get almost fifty thousand instead of thirty three thousand like I figured we'd get! What a pleasant surprise that is! Well, I'm on the highway right now, heading back home, so I can't talk for long. I just wanted you to know what's happening. Talk to you later." Before I could utter a word she hung up, leaving me stunned at her enthusiastic tone. Her tone was in such sharp contrast to the deep despair I was feeling that morning it was shocking. Her lack of empathy caused me to stop and think of how inappropriate it was for her to be so eager to file the insurance claim and get her hands on the money so soon after Sarah's death. Carla's insensitivity laid heavy on my mind and I couldn't help but think something was amiss but as always it was just a gut feeling with no proof of ill doing.

Sure enough, as promised, I received my check for forty-seven thousand dollars in the mail Monday morning. Wondering how the check could have been issued without my signature, I called the insurance company to enquire about it. After explaining my concern about the papers being signed by someone else without my permission the woman on the other end of the phone explained, very curtly, that all the proper information had been supplied to them and there was no reason not to process the claim. She continued by saying my check had been mailed out to me and the other two checks were handed over to Carla.

Then, she asked, "Did you not receive your check?"

"Yes I did." I answered.

"Well then, I don't see what the problem is." She answered back.

Perplexed about the lack of concern the insurance agent showed towards the enquiry I was making, I asked if I could have a copy of the insurance forms sent to me. I wanted to see the signature for myself. No doubt, if it had been anyone but Carla I may have not been so adamant about proving any wrong doing but I felt she had overstepped her bounds and I didn't want her to get into the habit of signing my name without my permission. I was hoping she would have to face some kind of consequence for taking it upon herself to sign without my say so.

Later in the week when I received the forms in the mail I could see someone had signed my name and Matt had witnessed it. I was so angry. Carla had gone ahead and signed my name without my permission after I'd clearly pointed out I wanted to know what I was signing my name to and asked her to mail the forms to me. Not only had someone signed my name but Matt witnessed it as being my signature. Wasn't that fraud?

Determined to bring this obvious loophole in their system to their attention, once again, I contacted the insurance company, spoke to their fraud department and explained my discovery, of what I thought to be a criminal act of fraud. The following day I received a call back from a representative from the fraud department. She introduced herself as the person appointed to investigate my complaint and after a long pause she clearly pointed out to me,

"I understand your concern but if we questioned every person who came in here with a claim, we'd never get any claims settled!"

I was stunned by her curtness and really didn't know how to respond to her obstinate answer. After hanging up I was feeling more confused than ever and was still left to wonder how Carla managed to get her hands on Mark's check. He certainly wasn't capable of signing for himself and she was in no way related to him nor was she his guardian, she was simply his paid caregiver. I guess being executor of Sarah's will was a very powerful card to hold. Even so, it just didn't seem right.

Eleven days after my sister's death, Carla left the insurance company with close to one hundred thousand dollars in checks and nobody was interested in looking into the possibility that an actual act of fraud had been committed to obtain them. My attempts to bring the facts to the proper authorities proved to be fruitless and I was left feeling as though I was the criminal for making enquiries. Stunned at the lack of interest shown by the insurance company I had no alternative but to just accept the unjustness of what had happened and get on with my life.

The memorial was only days away, so I made one more attempt in calling Carla to let her know I hadn't received a copy of the will yet.

"I really don't know what's happened to it." She replied. "I sent it a while back. You should have received it by now."

"Well, I haven't received anything in the mail. Could you send me another copy?" I requested.

"Sure, I'll send that out to you right away," she promised.

It seemed there was no end of things to take care of in preparation for Sarah's memorial. At last, it was time to set out our clothes for the following day and try to get some rest. Waking up early I lay there contemplating what the day had in store for us. Not looking forward to what lay ahead I started going through the motions of getting myself ready and filling the van with everything we'd offered to provide. We chose a lovely wooden urn to hold Sarah's ashes. A brass plaque engraved with a touching poem, appropriately called "Sarah*'s Smile*" was placed on the top lid. Doug meticulously crafted a beautiful wooden cross to be placed at the roadside. Embellished with fresh blossoms of red roses, off white calla lilies and the addition of a simple brass plaque, inscribed in Sarah's honor, you could see it was truly a labor of love. The candles decorated with delicate purple flowers and tied with a fine satin ribbon were individually wrapped in tissue paper and packed into a small wooden chest, ready to be handed out to everyone in attendance. Finally, with everything accounted for we started out.

I was oblivious to anything happening around me as we made our way along the highway. Thoughts and feelings seemed foreign as I fell into an intense state of mourning. It was incredibly difficult for me to accept I was on my way to attend my baby sister's memorial. Lamenting over what this day represented, tears flowed freely. Engulfed in sorrow I was relieved when we finally arrived at our destination. Once inside the house I noticed the tables and chairs were being set up and the Celebrant had arrived early to prepare the talk she planned to deliver during the service. After meeting with her and getting an idea of what she was going to present that day, I knew Sarah would be pleased with our decision of having a private ceremony.

We'd thought to rent a sound system and I was glad because even though the house had an open concept layout, it was a large area and people would be seated on two levels. The sound system would help make it possible for everyone to be able to hear the service. Doug busied himself with setting up the speakers while I showed the caterers where to set out the food. It was an elaborate buffet, donated by one of Sarah's friends. The florist finally arrived with a truck load of flowers. Red roses were Sarah's favorite, so we ordered fifteen dozen, long stemmed, red roses, placed them into vases and scattered them throughout the room. They were absolutely stunning.

As I was placing the floral arrangements around the room, Carla seemed to appear from nowhere and standing next to me she blurted out,

"I know Sarah stated in the will she wanted her remains donated to McMaster University but I had her cremated instead. I hope you don't mind?"

Then as quickly as she'd appeared she turned and I lost sight of her, leaving me to deal with the shock of her incomprehensible remark.

Did I hear her right? I asked myself in disbelief. *Do I mind if she had Sarah cremated, when her wishes were to have her body donated?* I repeated to myself. I then began to seethe. *How dare her go against Sarah's wishes? Who does that?* I continued to ask myself over and over again. With the addition of the final vase of roses the room I was decorating was complete and I was free to go in search of Doug to inform him of my latest encounter with Carla. I found him downstairs still setting up chairs. One look at me and he could see something was wrong.

"What's happening?" He enquired.

Once I'd finished explaining what had just transpired between Carla and I he was just as troubled by the situation as I was. We figured this is why Carla was so evasive about giving us a copy of the will and we wondered what other surprises were in store for us? We both agreed we needed to get a copy of the will ASAP! Doug was livid and went to look for Carla. When he caught up with her, he mentioned we hadn't received a copy of the will in the mail yet and insisted we have a copy before we head back home. He said he would drop by her place to get a copy from her the following day when we picked Mark up to take him back to stay with us while they travelled to China.

Carla tried telling him she'd been too busy and too distraught to even think about the will. She claimed she didn't have a copy because it was still at the lawyers. Doug realized these were out and out lies because he knew she had to have shown the funeral director the will as proof of being executor of the estate, and besides why would she promise us a copy was in the mail if she didn't have one. Ignoring her feeble attempts at putting us off, once again, he insisted in no uncertain terms, he have a copy in his hands before we leave to go home the following day. I just didn't understand. More lies, but why? What reason did she have to lie to us? Why would she have Sarah cremated against her wishes? We would have liked to get to the bottom of this but as much as we wanted answers this was not the time or place to try to get them.

Soon, the house began to fill up with Sarah's friends and family. They were all there to give their condolences and pay their respects to her memory. For much of the afternoon, I was plagued with grief and preoccupied with my own thoughts. Every so often, a rumor of Carla throwing Sarah a proper "send-off" that night at Sarah's house, passed my way, bringing me back to the reality and the disrespect Carla showed time and time again towards my sister. To me the idea of holding a party in the house Sarah so lovingly fashioned reeked of disrespect, leaving me feeling sick at heart.

When Carla began to give her eulogy I couldn't help but notice how hollow her words sounded. Void of emotion and without shedding a tear her message was clearly focused on how generous Sarah had been to her, mentioning numerous times that she referred to her as Mother Teresa and considered Carla to be her Guardian Angel. To tell the truth, the eulogy turned out to be more about how wonderful Carla was for being Sarah's friend than about Sarah. I thought I may have been imagining the coldness in her voice during her presentation but afterwards a number of people asked if I had noticed how unemotional Carla appeared, considering she claimed to be so close to Sarah. It was then I knew it wasn't just my imagination. After speaking, Carla presented a power point presentation in remembrance of Sarah. Played to the tune of Alan Jackson singing 'A Picture of Me Without You' there wasn't a dry eye in the house but still not a tear or sign of emotion from Carla.

Regardless of my disgust with Carla I felt Sarah was smiling down on us that day as the weather allowed the reception to spill out onto the deck and the surrounding gardens. When it came time for the roadside ceremony a small procession made its way to the spot where Doug, during the service, had gone to erect the cross on the exact spot where Sarah's SUV left the road. With roses in hand and candles lit the ceremony proceeded as planned.

Mark and I began by devoting a prayer to Sarah, a beautiful rendition of 'Amazing Grace' was played on someone's iPod and everything ended with the sound of Bette Midler singing one of Sarah's favorite songs 'The Rose'. Roses and candles were placed at the foot of the cross as the group broke up. It was a lovely little ceremony and I know Sarah would have approved. Afterward, a small group of close friends and family stayed behind to discuss the accident. Tire marks, still visible, marked out the final moments of Sarah's life. It was evident by the lengthy skid marks the brakes had locked as she tried to stop the vehicle. I stood there trying to imagine the scene. It must have been terrifying for her.

When we were leaving the ceremony Doug told me when he was there earlier positioning the cross, he went to the farm house next to the field where the accident had taken place to thank the people for calling 911 on the night of the accident. During the course of their conversation they told him there was a young woman who came knocking on their door to inform them she'd seen a truck leave the road and roll a number of times, ending up in their field. Apparently, the young woman couldn't wait and quickly left. While the wife called 911 the farmer hurried out to the scene of the accident where he found my sister's lifeless body. We thought it was strange to hear about this young girl actually witnessing the accident happen. This is the first time we were made aware of a witness.

The following morning I stayed behind with my friend. While taking our time over a second cup of coffee we caught up on the latest news. Meanwhile, Doug drove back to Carla's to pick up Mark and the will as promised. Doug arrived to find the party from the night before still in full swing. A glance into the smoke infested room showed whisky soaked mourners as they hung around each other's necks listening to some country singer wail out his sad tune. Carla suddenly appeared and promptly handed Doug a copy of the will as she pushed Mark, bags in hand, out the door. Hollering, she pointed out,

"He's got a thousand bucks on him. That should tide him over till we get back."

As we waved goodbye to our friends, thanking them for allowing us to stay with them Mark mentioned the Grey Cup game, which he never missed watching was on TV that afternoon. Knowing we wouldn't make it home in time to watch the game and knowing how much the Grey Cup finals meant to Mark we decided to visit my daughter, who lives in Cambridge, to see if we could watch the game on her TV. Mark was so excited about our change of plans. He loved his nieces and thoroughly enjoyed visiting them, so when we dropped in to watch the game he was more than happy. By halftime we were all getting pretty hungry and it was decided we would order a pizza. Mark, boasting about all the money he had said he wanted to pay which reminded us to get him to put his money somewhere safe. He emptied his pockets to a grand total of one hundred dollars. Doug and I looked at each other shaking our heads remembering Carla's claim of sending him off with a thousand bucks. We weren't surprised at the miscount.

We stayed for the entire game, so it was quite late by the time we arrived home. It felt good to finally be able to relax and put our feet up. The days leading up to and the day of the memorial itself were draining. There was no end of things to do in preparation for the day and now that it was over there was nothing to do but to find a way to carry on knowing Sarah was no longer here. It felt good having Mark with me during this time. He was the only immediate family I had left and I needed him to be with me right then. More than ever I realized how important it was to cherish our relationship.

It didn't take long for us to fall into our beds that evening. In the morning, once I had a chance to have a good look at Mark, I noticed he looked pretty shabby. His hair was uncut and greasy, the pants he was wearing looked like they were hand me downs from someone at least six inches taller than him, all tattered and torn from him walking on the bottoms of them and his well-worn, faded t-shirt sported a tacky brewery emblem on the front. In short, he looked like a bum, so a trip to the barber was planned as well as a day of shopping to replenish a well needed wardrobe for him.

Later that evening after his bath, Mark was trying on some of his new outfits when I happened to notice his toenails. I gasped in horror at the length of them. It must have been very painful for him to walk around like that. I became very concerned about the kind of care he was receiving from Carla. He certainly deserved better than this! After all, she was being paid very well to care for him. Mark was relieved when Doug offered to give him a much needed pedicure.

That evening after Mark had gone to bed Doug and I took the opportunity to open Sarah's will and carefully read it through. Each paragraph took me farther and farther into disbelief. I finally looked at Doug and exclaimed,

"I don't think Sarah wrote this! There are just too many loose ends! Nothing's specific! Sarah was too exacting to leave this, with so many errors and omissions, as her last will and testament. There's something very wrong here!" I exclaimed.

Doug was in agreement and said, "This just doesn't seem right, we'll have to look into it!"

Unsettled, after reading the will, we spent a restless night but when we heard Mark moving around in the early morning hours we got up. Once breakfast was finished and Mark had gone to his room to listen to the radio, Doug and I sat in the sunroom drinking our coffee. After we finished having our morning chat we decided to read the will over again, thinking somehow it would sit better with us in the daylight.

After carefully reading the will over for a second time, I was even more convinced these were not Sarah's final wishes. The first thing that struck me as being odd was the omission of Sarah's wishes for Mark's future care. Mark was one of Sarah's greatest concerns. It was unthinkable that she would have written a will without specifying her wishes for him after all she was very specific about Mark's care in her previous will.

Nor, was it like her not to mention her intentions for her business or the puppies. This was a sure giveaway that Sarah was not the one who wrote this will. The puppies were her life. I can't imagine her not being specific about how she wanted her puppies to be cared for. Her previous will had explicit instructions for the kennel. This will left no instructions for the kennel or her beloved puppies whatsoever.

When you look at paragraph III it states,

> "all the property, whatsoever situate, including any property over which I may have a general power of appointment... namely."

This statement is left incomplete, ending right in the middle of the sentence. She names none of her assets. In her previous will she mentions specific bank accounts and trust accounts including locations and holding institutions. This just didn't seem right. It made no sense to me at all.

Paragraph V states the estate is to be divided equally between Carla, Mark and myself. This is the only time mine and Mark's actual names were mentioned.

Paragraph VI of the will refers to Trusteeship, stating,

"if any person should become entitled to any share of my estate before attaining the age of majority or while mentally incapable of managing property, the share of such person shall be held by my trustees... while mentally incapable of managing property when such share or the amount thereof remaining shall be paid or transferred to him or her, or should such person die before attaining the age of majority or while mentally incapable of managing property, this share will be transferred to his or her legal representative."

The above paragraph left Carla in a position of extreme power over Mark if she were to gain guardianship over him. Carla was quite aware of Mark's trust money and she was in receipt of Mark's forty-seven thousand dollar check from Sarah's life insurance. It was wrong for Carla to assume this responsibility of Mark as she did not have guardianship of him and there was never an assessment done as to Mark's mental capabilities. Besides his name was not mentioned or referred to in this paragraph.

In Paragraph VII the will states,

> "I authorize my trustees to use their discretion in the realization of my estate, with power to sell, call in and convert into money any part of my estate not consisting of money at such time or times, in such manner and upon such terms and or for either cash or credit or for part cash

> and part credit as they may in their absolute discretion decide upon, or to postpone such conversion of my estate or any part or parts thereof for such length of time as they may think best. My trustees shall have a separate and substantive power to retain any of my investments or assets in the form existing at the date of my death at their absolute discretion without responsibility for loss to the intent that investments or assets so retained shall be deemed to be authorized investments for all purposes of this my will."

This paragraph gives the executor, namely Carla, the power to do what she wants whenever and however she pleases without holding any responsibility for her decisions. Under normal circumstances this paragraph would have been acceptable but in the hands of someone who was as deficient and immoral as I knew Carla to be, this statement was a license allowing her to rape the estate.

I thought it was very strange that paragraph XI and XII were completely missing. The Roman numerals were there but that was it, leaving me to wonder what was contained in these paragraphs? Is it even legal to just leave paragraphs out of a will?

In paragraph XIII Sarah states,

> I authorize my trustees to permit any of my physical organs to be used for the purpose of transplants and to permit the use of my body for the purposes of medical research and education. In particular, it is my desire that my body be donated to McMaster University.

The will clearly stated Sarah's wishes were to have her body donated for research and education and yet Carla had made the decision to have her cremated by the time we arrived at the funeral home on the morning after her death. Carla was involved when the will was being drawn up, so she would have been well aware of this direction. It hurt me to think she had so little regard for my sister that she would defy her final wishes. Questioning Carla's motive for withholding a copy of the will from me sent a chill down my spine.

As we looked closer we realized Carla's name was misspelled throughout the entire will. It showed her name as Carly not Carla. I was always under the impression wills were to be precise, no errors. Is the misspelling of a name on a legal document even legal? Besides, Sarah was too meticulous to allow the misspelling of Carla's name slip by her.

Also, the will refers to 'my trustees' repeatedly, indicating more than one trustee.

One last observation, even though just a small detail, there was no mention of Mark or I being

Sarah's next of kin. I always thought including next of kin was normal procedure in the writing of a will.

After dissecting the will for a second time I was positive Sarah had nothing to do with its' making. The entire document screamed of Carla. Lacking or vague at best, in specific names and instructions, as well as, issues that were paramount in Sarah's life, my suspicions were aroused once again. I felt this was not something Sarah would have allowed. She was far too meticulous to leave everything so up in the air. A second reading of the will only reaffirmed to me this was not Sarah's doing. I am not a lawyer but my gut instinct told me this will has been doctored. I will never accept these were Sarah's true wishes.

~ Chapter Eight ~

*"Honesty means standing up for what is right,
even if it means you stand alone."
~ Anonymous*

Carla, Matt and Jennifer left for China, on December 2, 2011 as planned. As for us, we stayed up half the night to watch a movie with Mark and were having a slow start to the day. While I nursed my second cup of coffee and was contemplating getting dressed the phone rang. Glancing at call display I could see it was from Warwick Association Family Respite Services, otherwise known as WAFRS.

Now, why on earth would they be calling? I wondered as I picked up.

It was one of Mark's respite workers from WAFRS, wanting to know if Doug and I could meet with them sometime before Carla returned from China. Taking me by surprise, she asked if we knew what was going on with Sarah's business and her estate, then without waiting for an answer or elaborating on the purpose of the meeting she asked if the 12th at 1 pm was O.K.? Agreeing to meet with them, she politely said they were looking forward to seeing us and hung up. I knew the call had been made by a coworker of Sarah's at WAFRS who continued to work with Mark to this day but I couldn't think of any reason why they would be concerned with Sarah's personal affairs. When Doug came in I mentioned the mysterious call I'd just received. We were both left wondering what could possibly be that important for them to ask us to make such a lengthy trip to meet with them and why they specified we meet before Carla returned from her trip on the 16th. We were completely puzzled.

While unpacking Mark's duffle bag he showed me the cell phone Carla had bought for him. He was very excited about it and pointed out the button he needed to press to get through to her. He pressed the button and almost immediately a call came in to him from Carla. That was the first of a constant stream of phone calls Carla supposedly made from China. She would call constantly during the day and well into the night to tell him how much she missed him and let him know of all the wonderful gifts she was promising to bring home for him. It was difficult for Mark to enjoy his time with us while he was kept distracted with her calls. I found it strange how, even in her absence, she managed to keep him focused on her. Mark's conversations were centered on all the wonderful things he would be showered with once Carla returned. Her calls bordered on harassment and I found them to be obsessive, intrusive, disruptive and unnecessary.

The following week I decided to track down the trust fund our mom set up for Mark before she passed away. Sarah was the trustee of this fund and I was appointed the alternate. This meant, if for any reason, Sarah was unable to fulfill her duties the responsibility of managing this fund would be passed down to me. I began my search by calling the Royal Bank of Canada where Sarah did her business. I remembered going to the bank with Sarah to open the trust there years ago. Amazingly, the woman I spoke to was the same person who originally set it up. Familiar with Sarah she was very surprised to hear the tragic news of her death and told me the bank hadn't been informed of her fatal accident. Apparently, any active accounts should have been closed from the moment of her passing. She asked me to stay on the line while she checked the records of Sarah's accounts. When she came back she asked if the name Matt rang a bell. When I told her he was the boyfriend of an employee Sarah had hired, she exclaimed,

"There may be criminal activity here!"

Then, she quickly informed me, unless I was the executor of Sarah's estate our conversation was over. After hanging up I sat there in disbelief, trying to figure out what had just happened. It was now December 5, five weeks after Sarah's accident and Carla, as the executor of her estate, hadn't informed the banks of her death. On top of that, what did Matt have to do with Sarah's banking? It was beyond me. I couldn't even begin to figure out what was going on but I really wasn't surprised to hear the two of them were involved. I was just glad the bank was finally aware of what was going on and I was sure they would be looking into things.

Regardless of feeling unsettled about this latest discovery at the bank and Carla's constant bombardment of phone calls to Mark, we did manage to enjoy our time together. Christmas was just around the corner and there was so much to do. Shopping and holiday concerts filled our days and nights with a rush of activity and I was thankful to have Mark to celebrate the season with us. His presence helped to fill the void I felt after losing Sarah.

The ever-present feeling of sorrow I'd been harboring was beginning to wane but with Christmas fast approaching it returned with a vengeance and once again became my constant companion. It followed me as I went through my daily routine and plagued me with sleepless nights, constantly reminding me of the emptiness in my life. At some point my grief had shifted from the sharp gripping waves of shock to the never ending drone of disbelief. Either way, it was relentless, making it difficult to manage my hectic days and even more difficult to make it through the long, painful nights.

Somehow the days slipped by and it was time to make the trip to meet with WAFRS. We were anxious to find out what this was all about. Two of Sarah's friends from WAFRS called to let us know the director of WAFRS would also be present and for some reason the venue for the meeting had been changed and we were advised we would be meeting at one of their homes rather than the association offices.

"It must be something really important for all of them to go out of their way to attend this meeting." Doug stated.

"I have no idea what it could be but it must be huge." I answered.

We'd made plans for Mark to stay with his niece Kellie, who lived close by the association offices while we attended the meeting. Mark was delighted to be able to spend the day with her and couldn't wait to see her. When we finally arrived at her place we had a short visit then Doug and I left, leaving the two of them to plan their day together.

The mystery behind this meeting remained with us as we arrived at our destination. Everyone was waiting inside when we knocked on the door and after introductions and being informed that one of them couldn't be there but would be kept up to date via blackberry we were ushered into the living room. First we were told they had all met earlier in the month, at the request of one of Sarah's close friends, and they felt we should be made aware of what took place during that meeting.

They continued, "As you know, Lynn is a fellow dog breeder and a good friend of Sarah's. She felt it necessary to share Carla's bizarre behavior that she witnessed after Sarah's death. She wasn't sure who to discuss this with so she contacted us at the association to set up an appointment knowing we were familiar with Mark and would have his best interest in mind. After we heard what she had to say we decided you and Doug should be made aware of how Carla is handling Sarah's estate."

Listening to what was being said, my mind flooded with all the distrust I harbored toward Carla. My suspicions were rekindled and my interest was sparked but I decided to keep my thoughts to myself until I'd heard everything they had to say.

The conversation continued, "Apparently, Lynn contacted Carla right after Sarah's accident. Being a close friend of Sarah's and a breeder of Maltese puppies herself, she was interested in the well-being of the orphaned pups. She found out Carla, with the help of Sarah's groomer, were continuing to care for the kennel, so, she paid a visit to offer her services. After what she witnessed and not knowing where else to turn she contacted us to set up a meeting to discuss what she felt was deviant behavior on the part of Carla. Because Mark is a client of ours and Sarah was a co-worker and good friend we all agreed to meet with her. During our meeting she discussed how the morning after Sarah was killed, Carla told her she went to the field where the accident had occurred. She said she was looking for any papers or cards the police may have missed. After that she drove to the place where Sarah's SUV had been towed and managed to get permission to search the vehicle."

I listened in horror, creating a mental picture of what it must have been like to search Sarah's vehicle and the area where Sarah had taken her last breath. From what I had been told Sarah had bled out and the scene was a bloody mess. I knew Carla was capable of just about anything but what kind of person would find it necessary to go to that extent? She really must have been looking for something specific. I shuddered as the conversation continued.

"Lynn claims Carla knew Sarah had been to the lawyers that morning to sign the final papers for the house and they were on the front seat of the truck when she crashed. Carla said they had blown all over the field but she was able to gather most of them up. That same day Carla was going through Sarah's mail and opened her bank statement. She said Carla was quite upset to see a negative balance when she knew Sarah had just deposited twenty-five thousand dollars into that account. Lynn took the statement from Carla and after looking it over showed her that she'd been looking at Sarah's checking and not her savings account. Turning the statement over it showed twenty-five thousand dollars had been deposited into Sarah's savings account just prior to her death. Carla claimed the lawyer had advised her to clean out all Sarah's accounts before she informed the banks of her death."

The longer the conversation went on the angrier I became. I really didn't know how to process what I was hearing, it almost sounded too macabre to be true. Feeling sick at heart the reality of Carla's actions following Sarah's accident were starting to sink in. The gasps coming from others in the room confirmed to me I wasn't the only one who found Carla's behavior questionable, leaving me with little doubt that things were not on the up and up and something underhanded actually was going on. Trying to sort through what I'd just been told, someone sitting in the room spoke up.

"Oh, and by the way, Lynn heard from one of the other dog breeders that Carla continued running the kennel like nothing had happened and didn't inform any of Sarah's business associates of her death."

At that point, I didn't think I could listen to another word of Carla's deplorable behavior. "What are we dealing with here, a psycho!?" I cried out not knowing how to process the words I was hearing.

I turned to Doug in a desperate attempt to get an answer to my question. It was at that moment we began to fear for Mark's safety and we both agreed there was no way he was ever going to return to Carla when she returned from vacation. We made the decision right then and there to keep him with us. After all, we were the only family he had left and we loved him dearly. With support through WAFRS we felt we should be able to manage. The concept of us bringing Mark to live with us permanently was a fresh, uncharted idea and regardless of having so many details to work out, we realized it was doable and everyone in the room agreed our decision was in Mark's best interest.

Now it was our turn to share the concerns we had about Carla's behavior. We began by explaining what a hard time we had getting Carla to hand over to us a copy of Sarah's will, adding, when we finally did receive it, it was clear Sarah's wishes were to have her body donated to McMaster University for research, but for whatever reason, Carla made the decision to have her cremated and didn't inform me of Sarah's actual wishes until the day of the memorial. I went on to tell them of my suspicions concerning the will being fraudulent. With that everyone gasped but as I continued to elaborate I had everyone's attention and you could have heard a pin drop in the room.

"It was December 5, five weeks after Sarah's death, when I tried to track down Mark's trust. I began my search by contacting the bank where the trust was set up years ago and managed to speak to the woman who actually set it up. Can you imagine she was still working there after all these years? She asked why I was enquiring about Mark's Trust and when I told her about Sarah she was surprised to hear of her tragic death. This was the first time she'd heard anything about it. It was now five weeks after Sarah's passing and Carla, as the executor of the will, still hadn't told the bank of her death. After checking into Sarah's records she returned to the phone and asked if the name Matt meant anything to me? When I told her who he was she commented about the possibility of there being criminal activity. When she realized I wasn't the executor of the will our conversation was over."

The room remained silent as I continued,

"It was only one week after Sarah's passing, on November 8, when Carla called to tell me she was putting in a claim for Sarah's life insurance and needed my permission for her to sign my name to the forms. She also needed my social insurance number. I didn't have a problem with giving her my SIN number but when it came to her signing my name I told her I wanted to know what I was signing my name to and asked her to send me the forms. Three days later Carla called to tell me my check was in the mail and sounded pretty excited that it was for more than she'd thought. I wanted to know how she managed to get the money without my signature, so I had the insurance company send me a copy of the forms. Sure enough, when I received the forms I saw someone had signed my name and Matt had witnessed it as my signature. On top of that she had managed to somehow get her hands on Mark's check. That day she left there with almost one hundred thousand dollars in her hand. I don't trust her as far as I can throw her!" I exclaimed.

Someone interrupted to ask if we were ready to have a break. By this point, we were all overwhelmed with the odd and bizarre circumstances involving Carla and welcomed a break from the intense conversation but our discussion continued right through to the time we returned to the livingroom. Once we were all seated again I felt I should tell them of Sarah's telephone call. So, I began,

"It was around the middle of October when Sarah called one evening to get my opinion on some things that were bothering her. She told me Carla was refusing to pay back five thousand dollars she had loaned Carla's son for a down payment on a house. Sarah said Carla insisted it was given to him as a wedding gift and says he doesn't have to pay it back. Sarah insisted this was not a gift. She also told me Carla was starting to speak on her behalf at the lawyer's office and felt she was twisting her words. She mentioned she felt Matt and Carla were somehow messing with her finances but didn't go into detail about what it was they were doing. I told her she needed to get rid of her and go to the police or a lawyer to see if there was something she could do about it. Then, after speaking to me she asked to speak to Doug and told him she was being followed by someone with their high beams on at night when she was travelling home and asked him what she could do about it. Doug told her to try to get their license plate number, so she could report it to the police and try to stay off the roads at night. Unfortunately, we are now living with terrible regret because we weren't more help to her when she reached out to us."

Completely overwhelmed, I didn't know where to begin to deal with the information that was presented that day. My mind reeled with disgust as I realized Carla was at the center of it all. There was something about hearing everything laid out so condensed and in a nutshell that hit home and made it real. Anger began to well up and I found myself wishing the meeting was over with.

After a long silence I said, "I just don't understand why Carla has to lie about everything. She's so deceitful. You can't believe a word she says. She even insists Mark's been under her care for over ten years. The truth is he's only been living in the trailer on her property for a year now. She didn't even know him ten years ago."

Mark's worker spoke up and said, "I had no idea he'd been living at Carla's at all. I was under the impression he just visited with her the odd time.

Whenever I visited Mark he was always at home with Sarah and besides all of his funding was sent directly to Sarah and was still being authorized by her. There was nothing to indicate he was living with Carla at all."

The meeting lasted all afternoon and continued well into the evening bringing up endless accounts of Carla's absurd behavior. We tried to make sense of it all; the vague mention of Sarah's family on the obituary, Carla's self-centered interview with the reporter, her conviction and using Mark to steal from Wal-mart while still claiming her innocence, the eight hundred dollar check mom had written out to her when she blamed Mark for having money taken from her purse, the fifteen hundred dollars mom paid her to replace a patio door, that didn't even exist and claiming Mark broke it, the expensive gifts Mark came home with after spending time with her, Robert's claims of her and Matt getting Sarah drunk and then getting her to write out a check to them for work already paid for, our concerns with Sarah's will and the shameless disrespect they showed Sarah and Mark. We set it all out on the table. In total disbelief at the seriousness of the information we shared with each other that day we were all dumbfounded. The sheer volume of deceit alone was almost too much to comprehend and left every person in that room shaken to their core as the meeting came to a close. By that time, we were all in agreement that Matt and Carla were up to no good and Mark was best to stay with us.

At the end of the evening we all exchanged contact numbers and promised to keep in close touch. Before leaving I was asked to sign forms to allow me to authorize any funding Carla was entitled to receive from WAFRS on Mark's behalf. Sarah had authorized these payments previously, now this responsibility was being handed over to me. I felt honored by the gesture.

Totally depleted, we left to gather Mark from his fun-filled day with his niece and headed down the highway towards home. Silence hung in the air for the entire trip and we remained deep in thought as we processed the discussion that day. As soon as Mark was settled into bed and we were in the privacy of our own room we were able to openly rehash the events of the meeting but after all was said and done, we had no idea of what to do with all this newly acquired information. The only thing we knew for sure was that Mark was not going to return to Carla's care.

From that day forward a good rapport and strong support system began to build between Doug and I and everyone present at the meeting. They were all in favor of our decision to keep Mark with us and emails and phone calls supporting our decision circulated within our little circle on a daily basis. We hoped together we would be able to get to the bottom of Carla's scam and eventually show her up for the criminal she really was.

There was something about getting everything out in the open that left me feeling empowered. I now knew Sarah's will left Carla with complete control over the estate and she was required to answer to no one. Even so, Mark and I were Sarah's next of kin and the will stated we were entitled to our equal share of the estate. After hearing Carla was continuing to run the business after Sarah's death, I was curious. I emailed Carla in China to enquire about the kennel, particularly the sale of the puppies. She mailed back saying the kennel was shut down and no puppies were being sold at this time. Knowing how deceitful she was I decided to set her up by sending a message using an alias name to Sarah's personal email, to ask about purchasing a puppy from the kennel. Within a few hours I received an answer back from Sarah's computer telling us to contact her, after she finished her holidays, to arrange something without a word of Sarah's death. It was business as usual, in fact, if I didn't know any better I'd think it was Sarah answering my request. That's when I knew she planned to disperse of the kennel, right from underneath Mark and me and because everything was left to her discretion there was absolutely nothing I could do about it.

Initially, we'd made plans to meet Carla after she landed at the airport in Toronto on the 16^{th,} to return Mark to her but after the meeting with WAFRS that all changed, besides Mark was expressing that he wished to stay with us. We knew we had to tread lightly with Carla knowing her vengeance and unstable behavior, so until we had time to arrange a legal plan for Mark, we agreed to have WAFRS send Carla an email explaining there would be no need to pick up Mark because he wanted to stay with us for an undetermined amount of time over the holidays. Immediately, after sending the email, Carla made a brash call to me, from China, to find out what was going on. She was very upset to think he wasn't being returned to her care the moment they arrived back home. Amid her hostility I tried to explain that we were really enjoying our time together and Mark really wanted to stay with us a little longer. Carla was beyond reasoning at this point and continued to yell accusations into the phone,

"You can't do this! You have no right!"

I questioned her explosive reaction to such a simple request. This only strengthened my opinion of her mental instability and bizarre behavior and when she told me they were flying home immediately from China, to find out what was going on, I knew we'd made the right decision to keep Mark with us.

Immediately, Carla booked an earlier flight getting her home only eight hours earlier than her original flight would have, which made no sense to me at all. After landing, she insisted on meeting with the Director of WAFRS to find out what was going on, so on her way home from the airport she dropped in to speak with him. Once she left, the director found it necessary to put me on alert to let me know she was livid about what had transpired in her absence. He referred to her as frantic and to tell you the truth he sounded a little shook up himself. He warned me that Carla's ire was not to be underestimated.

After hanging up the phone I sat with a cup of tea and allowed myself a few moments to mull things over in my mind. I was completely baffled by her bizarre reaction to such a simple request. Actually, from the time of our meeting with WAFRS on the 12th, I'd put a lot of thought into what came out on that day. Combined with what I already knew about Carla's odd, freakish and criminal behavior I couldn't help but think that Carla really did have something to do with Sarah's death.

Carla knew Sarah was in a weakened state and she knew exactly what to do to keep Sarah dependent upon her. Sarah was drawn into Carla's web of deceit allowing Carla to embed herself into every nook and cranny of her life. In the end, Carla managed to manipulate Sarah's personal affairs to suit her own advantage. Once Sarah gained her sobriety back and began to see through Carla's scams I believe she approached Carla about her suspicions and how disappointed she was in her unacceptable behavior.

At that point Sarah was worth more to Carla dead than alive. With Sarah out of the way she was able to zero in on Mark and what he had to offer her. Only now, it was me who was standing between her and the ability to have complete control over him. A fair amount of money was attached to Mark and Carla saw me as a threat to her diabolical plan. She felt she was losing control of the situation, hence, her ire toward me. Suddenly, I realized how Carla had perfectly orchestrated everything to her advantage and I saw clearly her true motives. Once her intentions came into full light I gave myself permission to despise her with a passion.

While speaking to WAFRS the following day, on the 17th, about Carla's unusual behavior they proposed to hold a meeting with a professional mediator. Doug and I agreed to attend the well intentioned meeting with Matt and Carla on December 20. Matt and Carla also agreed to attend. Surprisingly, at eleven o'clock that very evening Matt and Carla showed up at my front door with the police to have Mark removed from my care. When the officer asked Mark where he wanted to live he was quite clear in saying he wanted to stay with us. I was beside myself to think they would stoop to this level to gain possession of him. Their obvious desperation just didn't make sense especially since we already agreed to attend a meeting on the 20th, to try to sort things out. Bringing the police to my door to have Mark removed only further heightened my dispise for them. At that point I really didn't want either one of them to have any contact with Mark at all but after the officer agreed to remain in the sunroom while they met I reluctantly allowed them to speak with Mark for a few minutes.

After a short visit with Mark, Matt and Carla left but the officer stayed behind to speak to Doug and me. He pointed out to us how Mark insisted repeatedly that he wanted to stay with us when he was asked by Carla to leave with her. Then, the officer went on to explain how he managed to arrive at our place.

"Earlier this evening, Matt and Carla called the station asking for an officer to meet them at the Tim

Horton's in Fairport and I just happened to be the officer on duty. When I sat down with them at Timmy's they explained how they felt we were keeping Mark against his will and then showed me an undated slip of paper stating if anything were to happen to Sarah, she wanted Mark to go into their care. Apparently, it was signed but not dated. It looked like something they had just put together themselves on the drive down here, leading me to doubt its validity. I listened to them as they tried to convince me of their story, then, after telling them there was nothing I could do to help, I advised them to turn around and go home. When they drove off I decided to follow them and as they pulled up in front of your place I pulled up right behind them."

He went on to explain that during the meeting with them in the sunroom, Carla handed Mark a can of candy while commenting to the officer "You know you have to watch him with this stuff. He chokes on it." He felt that was an odd thing for her to say.

"Why would you give someone something if you thought they might choke on it?" He questioned.

When I told him Mark had never had a problem with choking, he felt she could be setting up an "alibi" and warned us not to let Mark out of our sight for one second. During the visit in the sunroom Carla told him about all the calls and emails sent back and forth over the past few weeks while they were in China. He shared his skepticism about them communicating at will from China,

"I don't know where they were, all that time, but they certainly weren't in China. There's no way you have the freedom to communicate like that in that country." He emphasized.

The officer's skepticism towards Matt and Carla's intentions helped to justify any suspicions I was feeling towards their unexpected intrusion. It was then I realized how vulnerable Mark was and I found myself feeling an overwhelming need to hold him close and protect him from harm. It became clear to me we needed to look into getting legal advice to see what options we had in securing responsibility for Mark. I wasted no time in obtaining a highly recommended lawyer in the area. There was a sense of urgency in my voice when I called his office the following morning, hoping to make an immediate appointment. Thank God, someone had just cancelled and there was an opening on December 21.

The 20^{th,} rolled around all too quickly, as everything seems to do in the weeks leading up to Christmas. We were up bright and early that morning to begin our trip for the greatly anticipated mediation meeting. Carla, showing up at my door with the police to remove Mark from my care, seemed to be the breaking point in me having any toleration for her or her antics. As we travelled, we tried to imagine what good could possibly come of this meeting? Rehashing the deceit we'd come to expect from Carla the idea of a productive meeting seemed like a complete waste of time. I'd had enough of her games, so by the time we arrived, I was on the defensive. I'd made up my mind. I did not want this disturbed woman involved in Mark's life at all and I doubted this meeting was going to change my opinion.

As soon as we were seated across the table from each other I felt my anger start to stir and the walls begin to go up. I was not open to accepting any suggestions about Mark restoring a relationship with these people. The mediator was trying her best to find a middle ground for us to agree on but my mind was closed to any suggestions. Far too much water had passed under the bridge for me to even consider accepting Carla back into our lives. There were just too many unanswered questions concerning Sarah's death and Carla's complete obsession with Mark. How could I possibly make amends with someone I was convinced had something to do with the death of my sister?

At some point, I told Carla her services were no longer required and when the mediator asked me to clarify exactly what I meant by that, I complied. I stood up, leaned right into Carla's face and bellowed, **"You're fired!"**

With that Carla jumped up out of her seat and began crying,

"You can't do that! I don't know what I'd do without Mark in my life! He is my world! I would come to Fairport and rent a place if it meant I could see him! Maybe we could share him!"

I wasn't impressed by her outrageous reaction as I sat back watching her rant. If anything it only proved to me how bizarre this whole situation was and reaffirmed my decision to cut her out of our lives.

The meeting went well into the evening and when we were asked to leave, so the custodian could lock up the building for the night, we continued our discussion out in the parking lot. It was very cold that night, so in order to arrive at some type of conclusion and, quite honestly to get warmed up, I agreed to allow Carla to meet with Mark the following week for a few hours. Later that evening back at home, with Carla's absurd reaction to being fired still fresh in my mind, I felt very uneasy about allowing her to have access to Mark. I immediately called the mediator to let her know I was reneging on the agreement to allow Carla to spend time with Mark and I felt quite justified in doing so.

~ Chapter Nine ~

*"Some people come into our lives as blessings.
Some people come into our lives as lessons."*
~ Mother Teresa

The echo of Carla's pleadings to have contact with Mark seemed to border on insanity. I just couldn't get the picture of her freakish behavior out of my mind. It was very disturbing and continued to haunt me for days, sending chills down my spine. Even though it was made quite clear how we stood on her having no access to Mark she was making it plain to us, through emails and phone calls, she was not about to go away any time soon. We were relieved when it was time to attend the lawyers' appointment. Entering the office with Mark at our side and all our unanswered questions we felt optimistic about securing his future. The lawyer was very patient as we explained the dilemma we were in, stressing Carla's role as a hired caregiver for Mark, as well as a hired employee of my sister's and executor of her will. After we finished giving him a brief summary of our concerns, we told him we were there to see about becoming Mark's power of attorney and to find out how we would go about contesting my sister's will. The lawyer took a moment to look at Mark, sitting in the corner, then he stated,

"Becoming someone's power of attorney is not something you ask to become. Power of attorney is something that has to be appointed by the person themselves and according to what I have observed, Mark does not have the mental capacity to appoint a power of attorney for himself."

We were very disappointed to hear what the lawyer was telling us and it certainly wasn't what we wanted to hear but the law is the law and we couldn't argue.

Next, we discussed the idea of contesting the will and after looking over the copy we'd brought with us, we were asked what a rough estimate of the value of Sarah's estate would be. Between the kennel and the few belongings she owned we roughly estimated the estate to be valued at about one hundred and fifty thousand dollars. We didn't know what to say about the house because technically it wasn't really Sarah's yet, but Carla mentioned, somewhere along the way, she was going to get possession of it. In that case you could add another two hundred thousand to the total, then after taking a moment to look over the papers we'd given him he explained.

"Judges really don't like to go against the wishes set out by a person in their will. It costs a great deal of money to contest a will and unless the estate is worth upwards of five hundred thousand, I wouldn't recommend going ahead with that. It would cost you far more to contest the will than what the estate is worth. It just wouldn't be worth it."

We were not impressed with what we were hearing but we had come for legal advice. Feeling confident he knew what he was talking about we accepted his word.

Realizing we had to do something to protect Mark from being taken advantage of, we asked if there was anything else that could be done. He asked us if we knew what Mark was worth, so, I explained to him.

"Mark has a trust worth about one hundred and thirty thousand set up for him by my mom, before she passed away but Sarah was overseeing the trust and I don't know exactly what it's worth today. Close to fifty thousand was paid out to Mark from Sarah's life insurance which I assume Carla has and I'm not sure what's left of that either. Plus there was his monthly disability check worth around eleven hundred monthly that Sarah gave signing authority over to Matt, plus his Individualized Government Funding worth twenty-four thousand five hundred annually."

After summing up Mark's financial situation, we were advised to make arrangements to have him assessed by a Government Certified Assessment Officer and gave us the name of someone he knew who would come right to our house to test Mark. He said this would protect us against anyone trying to get a hand on his finances. He also advised us to have all his assets turned over to the public guardian and trustee.

"That will secure his money until you set up a plan of action." The lawyer advised.

Before we left the office he mentioned Carla would need to keep us informed of the status of the estate, as both Mark and I were listed as one third beneficiaries.

Once we arrived home I put on a fresh pot of coffee while Doug and Mark went in to watch a game on TV. As I sat alone in the kitchen enjoying the silence I pulled out the paper from my pocket with the information that had been jotted down to contact the Assessment Officer. I dialed her number. I wasn't very hopeful in getting her to assess Mark before Christmas after all it was December 21. Most people were caught up in all the hustle and bustle of the season right now, so you can imagine how surprised I was when she agreed to come to see us the following day.

The coffee was brewing and the cookies were set out by the time she arrived. Anxiously I answered the door to a very pleasant older woman who promptly introduced herself as Marjorie Wilson. Once we were all seated at the table, Marjorie spoke to Mark in a very gentle tone as she interacted with small talk until she was sure he felt comfortable speaking to her. Once assured, she asked him if he minded answering some questions for her.

Ah wight den." He answered her enthusiastically.

Then, he asked, "Wobin tay wit me?"

"Yes, of course, Robin can stay." She cheerfully answered.

I was given a word of caution that I could only stay if I didn't interfere with the assessment and with that the session began after agreeing not to assist Mark.

During the entire time Mark would look to me when he was unsure of what to say. If he didn't know the answer he would tell Marjorie to "Ask Wobin, Wobin knows". It felt awkward for me to just sit there and watch him struggle through the experience of having to answer questions for himself without intervening. It became increasingly clear to me, as I watched their interaction, how dependant Mark was on others. The simplest things we take for granted are a challenge for him.

During the assessment Mark's shortcomings were identified. He wasn't able to identify coins, when asked to make change or dial 911 on his own and he didn't remember his address or phone number. In desperation he would turn to me for help in answering the questions and I would have to let him know he was on his own. Throughout my entire life I had been conditioned to rescue Mark from difficult situations and it was hard to sit back and allow him to stumble. That day I witnessed exactly how innocent, helpless and vulnerable Mark really was and I vowed I would always be there to protect him.

When Marjorie finished the session with Mark she promised to have a report sent out to us within the next few days. We chatted for a few minutes while we had our tea and both agreed, in light of the situation with Carla, how necessary it was to have something in place as soon as possible to protect Mark from her having access to his finances. The following day we received the results of the assessment and as we had suspected the assessment concluded it was necessary for decisions to be made on Mark's behalf, by a person who is authorized to do so.

It was Christmas Eve. The tree sparkled with lights, highlighting the presents sitting underneath waiting to be opened. The following morning, after opening our gifts, the house began to fill up with the smells of Christmas as the aroma of roast turkey combined with the sprinklings of savory spices mingled in the air. The table was beautifully set with the holiday linen and mom's good dishes that were saved for special occasions only. With the addition of carols playing softly in the background the house took on an air of festivity. Everything was picture perfect but a distinct feeling of emptiness surrounded the day. As we went through the motions of a typical Christmas Day we were aware of an ever present void. Christmas had always been Sarah's favorite time of year. She always said there was something magical about the season and I had to agree with her but this year the magic was missing.

Over the holidays Carla was relentless in making her presence known by constantly calling Mark on his cell phone. Letters and emails arrived daily addressed to Doug and me as she did her best to instill guilt in us for not allowing her to see Mark. I found all of this extremely troubling knowing I had fired her at the mediation meeting. I hoped she would just go away and leave us alone, but she didn't. She carried on as if nothing had happened. Regardless of her pathetic pleadings I stood my ground and refused to allow her to see him.

After the meeting we had with the mediator I realized how demented this woman actually was and now that I suspected her of having a part in Sarah's death I certainly wasn't going to allow Mark to have contact with her. There were just too many unanswered questions and far too much outlandish conduct. We felt the police should be made aware of her odd behavior. We would have loved to confront her about everything but at this point we doubted her ability to tell the truth, so for the time being we chose to hold back on confronting her until we spoke to the authorities.

On Boxing Day, Doug took Mark along with him to do some shopping. Mark loved spending time in the electronics department, so he was left there to browse while Doug did some shopping of his own. When Doug finished he went back to the electronics department to find Mark so they could check out. Sure enough, he found him absorbed in looking through the DVD's. When Doug approached him he noticed he was holding his coat closed, as if he was hiding something. When asked what was under his coat Mark insisted it was nothing. After Doug demanded to see what it was Mark finally agreed to open his jacket and show what he was hiding.

"Awight den!" Mark conceded as he sheepishly pulled out a DVD from under his coat.

When Doug told him to put it back, Mark refused by insisting,

"No! Carla says hide it!"

After much coaxing and convincing from Doug, Mark finally agreed to return the DVD to the shelf. When they arrived home Doug told me about the incident. This behavior was totally out of character for Mark. I had never known him to steal; at least not intentionally. He had always been very honest and had a great respect for the law. Immediately my thoughts turned to Carla. *Had she groomed him to steal? I wasn't surprised. I wouldn't put anything past her at this point.* It became clear to me how manipulative she could be in using his innocence and vulnerability to her own advantage. *Get Mark to do the stealing and if he gets caught she could just stand back and say "I didn't have anything to do with it. He's the one who stole."* That scenario would fit right into her claims of innocence in the Wal-mart caper. *Poor Mark,* I thought. *In a court of law he wouldn't stand a chance and she knew it.*

From the time Carla became involved in Sarah and Mark's lives there'd been a constant course of events that left doubt, uncertainty and concern in our minds. We had never been the suspicious type or the ones to point the finger at others, but in this case, there were just too many questionable situations in our lives. Time and time again our suspicions pointed directly to one person, Carla. Starting from the time she entered our lives right up to the present, Carla was the sole central figure involved in every deceptive situation we encountered. We were convinced the knowledge we had regarding Carla's bizarre acts of deceit warranted being brought to the attention of the officers who were investigating Sarah's accident. Considering everything, we felt there was enough evidence to, at least, have Carla investigated in regards to Sarah's death. As a result, Doug made plans to take the information we had to the OPP in Port Elgin.

The day before the New Year, armed with all the information we'd gathered regarding Carla, Doug made the 400km trip to Port Elgin, to present the OPP with what we felt, was incriminating evidence relating to my sister's death. When he arrived at the station and spoke to the detective on duty he was told the file had been tagged and they were not accepting any more evidence to do with Sarah's accident. Doug left the station in disbelief, giving me a call before he started his trip back home.

"You won't believe this! They told me Sarah's file has been tagged. Whatever that's supposed to mean! They're not accepting any more evidence? Unbelievable!" He exclaimed. Then in desperation he asked."What do we do now?"

Doug was left with no choice but to turn around and come home. He arrived home late that evening feeling very tired and totally defeated. We were very disappointed in the outcome of the trip. Our intent was to hand over the information we had to the police but now we were left confused and not knowing where to turn to next.

It was a joy to have Mark around and we were feeling optimistic about him living with us. This urged us to finish the second story of our house so he would have his own space. With that in mind plans were underway to renovate a new space for Mark to live. He was thrilled with the idea and was there to put in his list of wants and wishes as we started the renovation.

The following week we received a letter from the Public Guardian and Trustee to say they had processed our application for them to act as Mark's financial guardian and assured us his finances were now under their control. I felt so much better knowing his money was safe and secure. This action protected Mark against anyone getting control of his finances and left me with one less concern for him.

As we settled into the New Year, Carla's insistence on seeing Mark continued as my patience with her began to wear thin. I continually asked myself, *why couldn't this woman just go away? Why is she so insistent on seeing him? Mark was still telling her he wanted to stay with us, so why was she still trying to persuade him to live with her?* By now I was sure she was after the money that was attached to him. Over the years I'd been involved with enough of her scams to know her obsession with having control of Mark had very little to do with concern for his wellbeing and more to do with her need for control of him and his finances.

It was starting off to be a very cold and snowy January, making it necessary to shovel the driveway almost every day. Doug and Mark had been out shoveling and came in, out of the cold, to have a hot chocolate and get warmed up. While we all sat at the table talking Doug mentioned there was someone parked down the street, on the side of the road, facing the wrong way and if he didn't know any better he'd say they were watching our house. After questioning why anyone would have a reason to be watching us, we dismissed the idea out of our thoughts completely.

Surprisingly, two nights later when Doug opened the front door to let the cat in for the evening I heard him hollering, so I ran to see what all the commotion was about. I found him yelling at someone who was running down the road. Once the intruder ran out of sight we came inside. Looking at Doug I could see he was visibly shaken.

"What was that all about?" I enquired.

"When I opened the door I saw someone crouched down, in front of the porch, hiding in the bushes. I must have scared him off because he took off running and ran out of sight behind the garage next door." He excitedly told me.

We tried to connect this incident with what we thought earlier was someone watching the house. After a short discussion we agreed it was probably just a coincidence. The truth is, we really didn't know what to think about it, so we took the situation that evening as being a local prankster who had been scared off and wouldn't be back to bother us and the previous situation that afternoon of being watched by someone, we chalked up to our wild imaginations. We were comfortable with our conclusions until later in the week, we received a call from our neighbor. She told us when she got up around three the night before, to get a drink of water she noticed a small, red car pulling up in front of our house. She said someone got out, slowly walked around the house then got back in the car and left. Thinking this was strange she just wanted us to know what had happened.

With this latest bit of information we had to accept these were not unrelated random acts. Immediately our thoughts turned to Carla and we knew without a doubt she was behind it all. We tried to figure out her reasoning for doing this by asking ourselves, *what was she trying to prove? Was she trying to intimidate us?* We were bewildered about why she would want to have us watched. All we knew for certain was she wasn't happy at all about not being able to see Mark but we had made up our minds. Mark was going to remain with us and she was just going to have to accept that fact. At this point, we were well aware of the lengths Carla would go to get what she wanted. As far as we were concerned she was a liar, a thief and possibly a murderer and with those thoughts in mind we were prepared to withstand her bullying and remained steadfast in our decision of Mark. We refused to allow her to get to us. As long as we made sure the house was locked up securely and we kept Mark close at hand, we felt we had nothing to fear.

Calling the police to report the strange circumstances that had taken place that week certainly entered our minds but being as we lived in a small town we didn't want to bring attention to ourselves. We felt being aware of Carla's threatening behavior was all we needed to protect us from her wrath, so we chose to ignore her antics in the hope she would eventually get tired of trying to do whatever she was trying to do and just go away. Her latest show of bullishness only strengthened our belief that it was in Mark's best interest to not have contact with her.

~ Chapter Ten ~

"True peace is not merely the absence
of tension…it is the presence of justice."
~ Martin Luther King Jr.

The last time Mark was shopping with Doug he spotted a wrestling magazine he liked and Doug promised to buy it for him the next time they went to town. A few days later when it was announced he was going shopping and asked who would like to come, it didn't take long for Mark to get ready and head out the door, reminding Doug of his promise. I decided to remain behind to get caught up on some housework. It was January 8, when I stood there waving to them as they pulled out of the driveway unaware that, once again, my life was about to be forever changed.

They'd only been gone a couple of hours when the phone rang.

Doug's voice quivered as I heard him say, "I'm so sorry but he's gone!"

"Who's gone?" I questioned.

"Mark! Mark's missing!" He hollered out.

"What! What do you mean he's missing?"

In disbelief I listened as he began to explain, "As soon as we got here Mark wanted to look through the magazines so I left him there while I went to pick up a few groceries. I told him I'd only be a few minutes and not to go anywhere else until I came back. After picking up the groceries I went back to where I'd left him and he was gone. I thought he might have gone to the electronics so I searched over there but there was no sight of him."

My heart was pounding in my chest as I hung on to every word he was saying.

"That's when I searched through the whole store but no luck. He was nowhere to be found!"

My mind began to race as the seriousness of what Doug was telling me began to sink in. Mark was always so good at listening to what he was told. Normally he stayed close realizing his dependency on you. I'd never known him to wander off when we went shopping. Immediately I knew something was very wrong.

Doug continued, "I thought something may have caught his eye on the way into the store so I ran over to McDonald's at the edge of the parking lot to see if he might have sauntered over there. None of the staff had seen anyone resembling Mark's description so I hurried back to Wal-mart to speak to the manager. He called all the employees to the front of the store to see if anyone had noticed him or witnessed any unusual behavior but no one had seen anything. That's when the manager decided to call the police. In fact, they're here right now and I'm being kept for questioning. I think I'm their number one suspect, seeing as I was the last one to be with him. I have to go right now. They want to speak to me. I'll keep you posted. I'm so sorry Robin."

By the time we hung up my mind was already connecting the strange events of the past week with what was happening now. *Oh, my God!* My mind screamed as I stood there trembling while my worst nightmare began to unfold before me. *Just as I suspected, we were being watched and stalked. They were just waiting for the opportune time to grab Mark.* I suddenly felt completely violated and filled with rage thinking back to all of the warning signs earlier in the week and I became visibly shaken at the thoughts of someone sneaking around watching us. I don't know if I was angrier at myself for underestimating the depths of Carla's deviant mind by ignoring the obvious red flags or the fact Carla would stoop so low as to kidnap Mark from us.

A sudden knock at the door brought me back to reality. When I opened the door an officer was standing there. I knew exactly why he was there, so I invited him in and once we were seated comfortably he asked if I minded answering a few questions in regards to Mark. The first question he asked was if I knew of anyone who would have wanted to take Mark or harm him in any way. Without giving it a second thought I blurted out Carla's name,

"And who is this Carla and why do you think she would be interested in your brother?"

I just couldn't get things out fast enough as I let him in on all my suspicions.

"Carla is a caregiver my sister Sarah hired in 2004 to take care of our brother, Mark, who is mentally handicapped. Over the past eight years I've watched as Carla and her partner drained my sister dry financially. In 2006 Carla was convicted of using my brother to steal from Wal-mart. She blamed him for the theft back then and still blames him for it to this day, even though she was convicted in a court of law.

I paused to take a breath and when the officer looked up from his notes I continued. "Somehow she managed to gain my sisters loyalty and Sarah ended up paying for all of her legal fees and her pardon out of Mark's trust. Over the years this woman managed to completely embed herself into my sister's life. Last year Sarah made Carla executor of her will. Sarah was killed in a single vehicle accident two months ago, so I brought my brother to stay with me afterwards."

I could tell the officer was struggling to keep with me and all the details but I was frantic about Mark, so I kept going. "Since then Carla has been trying to take him from me. She even showed up on my doorstep, with the police, at 11:00 at night, on December 17, to have him removed from my care. She said we were keeping Mark against his will but Mark told the officer he wanted to stay with us. The officer didn't remove Mark and after Matt and Carla left the officer remained behind to speak to us."

I paused for a moment to organize my thoughts, then, I began. “He told us he thought there was something strange about her behavior and not to let Mark out of our sight for a minute. From that time on she’s been constantly calling to speak to Mark and emailing me, asking to see him, even though I fired her at a meeting, on December 20. I could go on and on about the things Carla has done but it would take all day to explain it all to you. I wish that woman would just go away and leave us alone and that’s pretty much everything in a nutshell.” I concluded

Telling him everything didn’t make me feel any better but it certainly helped to put things in their proper perspective.

“And where does Carla live?” He asked.

“She’s lives a good four hours drive away from here but I’m sure she arranged for someone in this area to watch us this past week. We noticed someone watching us in a parked car, just down the road and we thought that was odd, then, a few nights later, Doug opened the front door to find someone hiding in the bushes but they ran away. Also, our neighbor witnessed someone parking their car, getting out and walking around our house at three in the morning. We didn’t know what to make of it at the time but now it all makes sense.”

“Did you report any of the events of this past week to the police? He asked.

“No we didn’t. We figured it all had something to do with Carla but we certainly didn’t expect her to stoop to this.”

"Well, it's too bad you didn't report it. You know, from what you're telling me, my guess is we're probably dealing with a predator."

"A predator?" I questioned. "I don't know exactly what that is but by the sounds of it the name seems to fit."

"Ya, we deal with her kind all the time. They prey on the weak and the vulnerable. It sounds to me like your sister was vulnerable and of course Mark goes without saying."

Just then, the phone rang. I asked the officer to excuse me while I answered. It was Doug calling to let me know what was happening with the investigation. Sounding very anxious he explained to me,

"I only have a few minutes so I'm going to try to bring you up to date on everything that's going on here. Right now I'm in the offices of Wal-mart with the detectives. They're questioning me about Mark. They've called in a team to do an extensive search of the building and the surrounding area and they've asked me to help them go through store video tapes from the time we arrived here. We had a real hard time identifying Mark leaving and they think he may have been disguised. I recognized someone leaving the building that looked like Mark but he wasn't wearing the same jacket he came in with. He was being escorted out of the store by some guy with his arms around him and both of their heads were bent down, so it was difficult to see their faces. The police pulled up the audio on the video and heard this guy telling Mark that Carla had presents for him and asked if he'd like to go see Carla? Of course Mark was more than willing to go with him. You know how easily Mark can be swayed if you offer him something he's interested in and presents would be right up his alley. Can you imagine it was only eleven minutes after we arrived here when this guy left the store with him? I told the police they're wasting their time looking for him around here. They need to be checking out Carla's house. Sorry Robin, but it looks like I have to go right now. The detective wants to speak to me. I'll call you later when I know more about what's going on. Love you."

After hanging up I returned to the kitchen to find the officer finishing up with taking his notes and before he put his notebook away he asked if there was anything else I wanted him to know.

"There is one more thing. I think you're wasting your time looking for him around here. You should be looking for him at Carla's place. I'm sure he'll show up at her place sooner or later." I answered, echoing Doug's words.

He nodded his head as if to agree with me, then, he let himself out.

Sitting at my computer I put out an all alerts bulletin to the kids and my newfound friends and support team at WAFRS, telling them about what was happening, in hopes of receiving some reassurance that eventually everything would work out fine. As I sat there in the silence, my first reaction was one of disgust at what was taking place and despise for the woman I was certain was responsible for kidnapping my brother and possibly killing my sister but more importantly I was feeling angry towards myself for not keeping my guard up and trivializing what this woman was capable of. My mind was chaotic with the uncertainty of the outcome of this situation but the one thing that was perfectly clear to me was that Carla was the person behind this deplorable act.

This seemed the appropriate time for me to close my eyes to take some time in prayer. Prayer offered me a peaceful retreat from all the chaos whirling around in our lives right then. Normally I gained a great deal of comfort from prayer but sure enough as soon as my eyes were open, the questions remained in my mind, nagging at me, waiting to be answered. *What kind of evil person is this woman? She had actually planned and schemed to take Mark away from us. She even had someone watch us, waiting for the perfect moment to pounce.* I shuddered to think of the depth of perversion in her twisted thinking.

I thought back to when the officer referred to her as a predator and thought to myself. *To my way of thinking, the label of predator seemed to fit her perfectly. From the time this woman entered our lives I had witnessed her preying on Sarah and Mark's finances and vulnerabilities. I'd even witnessed her prey on my mom, as she lay in her most vulnerable state on her death bed. This woman is despicable, has no compassion for anyone and is capable of just about anything. She is pure evil!* I concluded.

I sat there deep in thought and don't know how much time had passed before I was startled by Doug coming in. Relieved he was finally home, I put the kettle on and we both sat down with a cup of tea while he filled me in on what had transpired with Mark's investigation since I spoke to him last. Listening to him I tried to process his every word.

"I didn't want to leave the investigation until Mark was found." Doug remarked. "They were beginning to search the side of the highways and I knew I was a suspect. The reason I stayed there is because I wanted to be there in case they found his body. They sent police to wait outside Carla's place and about three hours after he was taken from Wal-mart some guy walked in her front door with Mark by his side. Immediately the police entered her house and began questioning everyone. Apparently, Carla claims she knew nothing about it. She denies knowing this guy but says Mark knows him from summer camp. Likely story that is, but the police at that end in Carla's jurisdiction didn't feel Mark was in any kind of danger so they allowed him to stay with her." I was left to wonder if Carla didn't have some kind of pull with the police at that end being as her son was a cop.

"How could something like this happen?" I cried in disbelief. "How can someone just steal your brother from you and get away with it? How could they let him stay with the very person who abducted him? I hope they don't believe her story of not knowing anything. It just doesn't make sense!" I was heartbroken.

The remainder of our conversation centered on rehashing the warning signs of the past week which, in hindsight, were so clear. Doug assured me it was not over yet as he explained an investigation was still in the works. Sleep did not come easily that night. My worst nightmare had been realized.

The following morning, I was jarred awake by the phone ringing. It was the detective from the police department. He wanted to make an appointment for us to meet with him that evening to discuss the details of Mark's disappearance. Arrangements were made for us to meet him at the station at seven o'clock that evening.

That day was a living nightmare trying to function in the depths of defeat as my thoughts remained focused on Mark. *Surely they won't allow Mark to remain with her when it was so obvious what she had done. They must be able to see through her lies. How could anyone think she didn't know anything about his abduction? It's so plain to see she's been planning this for some time now. She had us watched for God's sake. That has to be illegal.* The insanity of it all continued to engulf my thinking every moment of that day.

That evening, sitting in the office waiting for the detective to arrive, we had no idea what was about to take place. He finally came through the door flashing his ID and saying, "Hi, Detective Garrett here." Then after introducing ourselves, he asked if we objected to having our interview videotaped. Of course we agreed to be taped. We had nothing to hide and if it would help to clarify what was going on we were all for it. The detective had obviously been briefed about the background of this case and had read all the police reports that were written up.

He began by asking us to explain our take on the whole situation. In order for him to fully understand we were forced to go back over the years, once more, pointing out Carla's significance in all this. Beginning by telling him of our initial meeting with Carla and our suspicions of the expensive jacket she supposedly bought for Mark. We explained the years of deceit and denial and how she managed to embed herself into Sarah and Mark's life. How she drained my sister dry financially and blamed Mark for everything. How she gained my sister's trust and was made executor of her will. How we doubted the validity of the will and how she didn't report the death of my sister to the banks, the meeting with the mediator and how she came right to our door and tried to take Mark from us before Christmas. I emphasized how determined she was to have Mark in her care even after I fired her and if that wasn't enough we detailed the unusual events of the past week.

After giving what we felt was a fairly accurate account of things, he mentioned a name and asked if this name meant anything to us. After telling him the name Jack Cramer had no meaning to either of us he went on to explain,

"This is the name of the man who took Mark from Wal-mart and walked into Carla's with him, hours later."

Then he was interested in knowing if Doug would be able to identify the man hiding in the bushes earlier that week because we hadn't notified the police of the incident and it would help our case if he could. After trying to recall any defining characteristics of the culprit, Doug was eventually resigned to say,

"It was dark and it all happened so fast. He was gone before I knew what was happening. Sorry, I can't help you."

As the meeting came to a close we were warned our story may be taken as sour grapes by the District Attorney.

"Sour grapes! Are you kidding me? How could anyone even think that! Mark is my brother and he was intentionally taken from us! It's obvious it was all premeditated!" I exclaimed.

We left the interview that evening not sure of what kind of impression we'd left on the detective. All we knew for sure was that we had told the truth and really that was all we could do but we had no control over how that would be interpreted.

The following day the tears began and never stopped as the seriousness of this whole ordeal began to sink in. The mere fact my heartfelt sentiments could be misconscrued as sour grapes was unbelievable to me. Couldn't they see I wasn't the one who showed all the questionable behavior? Everything that was happening reverted back to Carla. How dare they even think it was sour grapes on my part! That woman had victimized my family for years and the mere thought of what was happening now left me feeling re-victimized and vulnerable to her distorted view of reality.

I know it was important to remain rational, especially when speaking to anyone of authority. Bitterness was viewed as a character fault but after witnessing Carla evade the law by her lies and deceit all these years it was a near impossibility to contain my ire towards her.

As the day wore on my feelings of anxiety reached unprecedented levels while waiting to hear from the detective. Today was the day a decision was to be made concerning the fate of Mark. Today a decision was to be made whether Mark would remain under Carla's care or be returned to us. Also, the decision concerning the guilt or innocence of Mark's abductor was to be dealt with today. The answers to those questions seemed clear to me but I needed to wait and hear the decision of the powers that be.

That afternoon Detective Garrett called to make arrangements to see us that evening at the station. I could hardly stand the uncertainty as we waited until 8 pm that evening to see him. We arrived early and sat anxiously in wait of the verdict. When Garrett finally walked in he sat down and explained Carla's take on how Mark came to end up at her place, we sat glued to his every word.

"Carla claims she does not know and has never even heard of Jack Cramer. On the other hand Jack Cramer says he was visiting with a friend of his in Clinton and coincidentally happened to bump into Mark while they were shopping in Wal-mart. He says Mark recognized him from summer camp and asked him to take him to see Carla. Jack put Mark in his car without notifying anyone and drove him right to Carla's house. The district Attorney has decided not to press charges against him or return Mark to your care because they feel he's not at risk where he is. Besides they say this is a civil case, not a criminal case, it's, you know, a family matter."

"What! I cried out. "You're trying to tell me they believed that cockamamie story they made up? That whole abduction was planned. What's wrong with them? There was nothing coincidental about it!"

"The DA is saying Mark went willingly when he was approached by Cramer." Detective Garrett replied.

"Don't you understand? Mark isn't capable of making a decision like that!" Then, remembering the words the police caught on audio in Wal-mart, I added, "He was bribed with presents. He'd follow you to the end of the earth and back if you offered him a Happy Meal let alone presents! What's wrong with you people?!" I retaliated.

"Well, as much as I can sympathize with you and as much as I argued the point with them, that's the decision the DA has made and they're sticking to it. There's nothing I can do about it. Their decision is final." We immediately got up and left. Partway down the hallway he shouted out to us from the doorway "Anyway, what does it matter if Mark ends up living in a shithole? Do you really think he'd know the difference?"

I really didn't know how to respond to the detective's summation of the situation, so I bit my tongue and just kept walking, my anger and bitterness increasing with every step I took. *How could someone in his position be that ignorant of the fact that Mark was a real human being with wants and needs and feelings just like the rest of us? Obviously he felt Mark's mental disability implied he wasn't deserving of being treated with dignity.* I was livid by the time I got home to think the detective felt his attitude towards Mark was, in any way, acceptable.

Playing the events of our meeting over and over in my mind only left me more disheartened than ever. *Clearly, Jack Cramer was a low-life who was asked to cowardly stalk us with the intent of taking Mark. I was already aware of the depths of evil Carla was capable of doing, but what I didn't understand was the DA looking at this whole situation and not seeing it as anything but a criminal act. It was obvious from the facts, it was planned and premeditated! Carla was Mark's caregiver, hired to look after him by my sister, my sister was killed and is no longer here, I fired her and she abducted him from me. She is not family! This is not a family matter! Why couldn't anyone see what was happening here?*

I was left to give the circumstances of Mark's abduction a lot of thought and couldn't understand how anyone could see what had taken place as anything but a deliberate criminal act. I decided to place a call to the detective and left a message for him to call me back. When he returned my call I desperately tried to emphasize how senseless their stories were.

Pointedly, I took the opportunity to run my queries past him, so I inquired.

"If this guy didn't know Carla, then how did he know where to take Mark? Wouldn't he have tried to find out why Mark was in Wal-mart alone and wouldn't it be only natural to find out if Mark was with anyone before he drove him four hundred kilometers away to Carla's? Carla's not even related to Mark, she was just his caregiver. I fired her and she deliberately had us stalked! Don't you see?" I cried out but the more I pointed out the obvious, the more I realized my words were falling on deaf ears.

At that point Garrett stopped me and said, "Look, I want to make something very clear to you; the DA had made up their minds and they are not about to change their decision. They feel this case is a civil case not a criminal case. End of story."

I hung up that day feeling totally helpless not knowing where to turn to next. To this day their decision to allow Mark to remain in the care of the very person who obviously had a hand in taking him from us boggles my mind and I am left wondering if Mark wasn't mentally handicapped, would he be receiving the same dismissive treatment?

~ Chapter Eleven ~

"You can close your eyes to the things you don't want to see but you can't close your heart to the things you don't want to feel."
~Johnny Depp

Once again, I was jarred into a living hell where the reality of my waking hours became surreal. The lingering grief from the loss of Sarah only two months before, coupled with the shock of having Mark suddenly snatched from my life took me into an unimaginable state of desperation. I felt as if someone had poured vinegar on the open wounds of my heart as I faced the possibility of losing my brother, as well. Distraught, angry and bitter over the lack of interest and common sense the D.A.'s office had shown by allowing Mark to remain in the care of the very woman who abducted him from his family stripped me of any hope I held of justice being served. I felt defeated. Oh, how I despised that woman! The mere thought of her sent my mind spiraling into a vile cesspool of nefarious thought. Witnessing years of her lies and deceit and knowing what I know now only served to increase my suspicions of her involvement in Sarah's death. I felt there was no limit to what this woman was capable of and I was left fearing for Mark's safety.

One afternoon, a few days after Mark's abduction, the phone rang. It was my cousin Danny.

"Hi Danny, how are you doing? I haven't seen you since the day of Sarah's memorial. What can I do for you?"

"I need to ask you a question. Who is this Carla?" He inquired.

"Why do you ask?"

"Well, the past couple of days she's been e-mailing me wanting to get together sometime and asking if I know your mom's maiden name." He explained.

"Oh no, I hope you didn't tell her."

"I couldn't tell her. I don't know what your mom's maiden name was." He replied.

"I have no idea of what she's up to Danny but if it was me I'd stay away from her. Trust me, she's evil! You realize she kidnapped Mark from us this past week, don't you?"

"Ya, I heard. It sounds like she's a real nutcase." He replied.

"She is. By the way, how did she get your e-mail address?"

"She went around at the memorial asking everyone in the family to give their address to her." He answered.

"You've got to be kidding! That means she was scheming even on the day of Sarah's memorial. What a devious little witch she really is!" I commented.

He explained, "You know, I usually don't like to get involved in things like this but when she was asking around for your mom's maiden name I thought I should let you know what she was up to. It seemed kind of creepy to me."

"Thanks for letting me know Danny and if you hear anything else please give me a call. We'll talk soon and remember; stay away from her! She's dangerous!" I emphasized.

This latest information from Danny left me trying to figure out what Carla was up to now. For the life of me I couldn't understand why she would need to know my mother's maiden name but from what I'd learned from past experience is that she never did anything without an ulterior motive. So here I was, once again, preoccupied with trying to make sense out of her nonsense. Confusion and chaos seemed to surround this woman and as much as I would have liked to eliminate her from our lives for good, she had possession of Mark, so I had no choice but to stay involved if I wanted to stay in touch with him and try to stay on top of her shady schemes.

That day my curiosity got the better of me when I decided to pull up Carla's face book page. I was interested in knowing a little more about her and hoped her profile would tell me something I wasn't aware of. Her profile showed she referred to herself as a 'Person of Influence' which I felt was a fairly accurate description of her, considering what a bully she is. I was casually looking over her page when I spotted Jack Cramer's name on her list of friends.

Just as I thought, they are friends or I should say more like partners in crime. It wasn't exactly a surprise to find out they did know each other after claiming to the police they didn't.

After years of observing Carla's devious behavior it irked me to see her literally get away with murder. From what I could see, she stopped at nothing to get what she wanted and somehow, somewhere along the line, I found myself obsessed with proving her lies. I felt if I dug deep enough the truth would begin to surface. I thought keeping a record of her blatant criminal behavior may prove to be useful if we ever ended up in court. If a person's character held any weight in who would be appointed Mark's guardian I felt if the truth came out about Carla we would win hands down, so, I began digging.

She must have known I was snooping around her site because within minutes of my discovery Cramer's name disappeared from her list and I was blocked from her site. At least now I knew they weren't strangers regardless of what they claimed. The satisfaction I felt uncovering their little secret was almost shameful. I reveled in the thought of her knowing she had overlooked something that could incriminate her and could only imagine her agonizing over that little slip up. The best part of it all was she knew I knew, but in reality, it was little compensation for the price Mark was paying.

Once Doug arrived home I told him about the call from Danny and my discovery of the abductor's name on Carla's face book. We both knew there was a real urgency in having Mark removed from her care and we needed to find a lawyer to begin proceedings to gain guardianship of him. We decided on the lawyer who wrote up our mother's will and who had set up a Henson Trust for Mark. Henson Trusts were a way for people on a disability pension to legally inherit money. Because this lawyer was instrumental in the development of the Henson Trust we felt he was a good choice. One phone call later we had an appointment with him.

We agreed upon a conference call to help speed up the process. After discussing the details of the guardianship and coming up with a plan of action I decided to mention the call from Danny. Curious to know why Carla would be interested in obtaining my mother's maiden name I asked if he had any ideas. Immediately, he pointed out, " it's probably one of two things. It's a password she needs to access one of Sarah's bank accounts or she needs to gain access to a safety deposit box.

"Of course, I should have guessed! It was a password!" I exclaimed.

Finding the answer to why she needed to know my mom's maiden name only brought up more unanswered questions and left me more confused than ever. One thing I did know for sure was her knowing the password would be of benefit to Carla and most likely end up cutting Mark and I out of our fair share of the estate.

Our initial meeting proved to be very productive as documents were filled out to begin the process of us gaining guardianship of Mark. The lawyer also directed us to have another assessment done on him, this time by an assessment officer of his choice. Once we decided on a time and place he would set a meeting up. The problem with that request was that we needed Mark to be present and I knew Carla would never allow us to have him assessed. She wasn't allowing Mark to be taken off her property and for us to be allowed to see him she was insisting on supervised visits, at her place, with her present. Right now she had complete control of Mark and she wasn't about to take any chances of compromising her sole authority. We would have to give serious consideration to how we were going to pry Mark away from her long enough to have him assessed.

After hanging up the phone I looked over at Doug who was sitting off to the side deep in thought. When I enquired what was on his mind he replied,

"I hope you realize she's going to run the whole estate down. She's going to clean out all the bank accounts and leave the estate worthless. She'll sell all the puppies and get rid of the business making sure you don't see one cent from that part of your inheritance and she'll do it just because she can. She's been working at getting into this position for a long time now, long before Sarah's death. Look at how she was taking advantage of her and robbing her blind all those years and now she's managed to get herself in a position to prey on Mark for everything he's worth! She's right where she wants to be."

As much as I didn't want to believe it, I knew what he was saying was true. Then, my thoughts turned to Mark. *Poor unsuspecting Mark,* I thought to myself, *he doesn't stand a chance against her.*

From the time we received a copy of Sarah's will we already suspected Carla of having a hand in its pro-executor creation and I knew from that moment on she was not about to allow me or Mark to receive what we were entitled to. I honestly felt Sarah didn't owe me a thing and if Carla thought she was deserving of my portion I could live with that but I hoped she would at least have the decency to make sure Mark received his fair share. Unfortunately, I knew deep down inside she only viewed Mark as another vulnerable victim to prey on. Knowing the depth of her moral corruption I swore I would do everything in my power to save him from her greedy clutches and make sure he received what was rightfully his.

Keeping in touch with Mark was made very difficult. Carla insisted the only way she would allow us to see him is if we agreed to visits at her home, with her present. I just couldn't imagine how that would all play out and could not bring myself to comply with her spiteful demands. This left us with contact by phone as our only means of staying in touch. What I didn't count on was having her present, on the other end of the line, during our private conversations. During each and every call I made to him she could be heard in the background coaching him on what to say and silencing him if he said something she didn't want him to tell me. Right out of the blue Mark began insisting he was not coming to visit with us until after court was over and he began asking me what I did with all his money. I knew these weren't his words. I could hear her prompting him and it was pathetic to hear how confused he would become trying to keep up with all her directions. Mark was difficult enough to understand as it was but when he became frustrated it was impossible to continue on with our conversations. It was obvious she was filling his head with ideas about us that were simply not true and it was disturbing when I began to hear word from his worker that she was telling them how stressful it was for Mark when he talked to me on the phone. Disturbing but not surprising, it was just like her to twist the truth to her advantage.

At the same time, I was hoping to be able to arrange visits with Mark without her being present. I refused to visit with him at Carla's with her in attendance, so I began e-mailing her trying to sway her into allowing us to take him out for dinner or at least have arranged visits with him at his niece's place, who lived close by. Finally, Carla agreed to an off premise visit only if she was allowed to attend with him. I continued to refuse to allow her to intrude on our family time together and eventually she agreed to an unsupervised visit at Mark's niece's home. Arrangements were made for Carla to bring him for a two hour visit. She insisted on waiting outside, in her vehicle, until our visit was finished. Regardless of being made to feel like criminals we agreed to her terms. After having two visits, at Kellie's place, where Carla waited outside in her vehicle the entire time, I had to ask myself. *Why is she so obsessed with having complete control of him? It just isn't normal to go to this extent!*

After tracking down the trust fund my mom had set up for Mark I found it was now being held by a financial institution and was being managed by a financial advisor. The trust was set up with me being appointed the alternate in case Sarah was not able to fulfill her responsibilities as trustee. To make the necessary changes to the trust, after Sarah's death, an original death certificate was required from Carla. A letter requesting this document was sent to her lawyer.

Later in the week I unexpectedly received a letter from Carla's lawyer. Curious to know what it could possibly be about I quickly opened it. I just couldn't believe my eyes. Carla was enquiring about all the jewelry and all the antiques I had removed from Sarah's house on November 2. I was stunned. There was an underlying insinuation I had stolen these articles without her permission. I was furious to think she was accusing me of stealing when the fact was she stood right there watching and told me to take whatever I wanted and said she wouldn't fight me for anything I took. I couldn't believe the level she'd stooped to this time. I only wanted the family jewelry and a few personal items belonging to Sarah and as far as antiques go there were no antiques unless you considered my grandfather's tool chest an antique. What right did she have to these things anyways? They were all family possessions. I turned furious at the accusation. Immediately, I searched for the bags of jewelry and when I brought them into the kitchen I dumped them out on the table. After removing the heirlooms I wrapped up the costume jewelry and mailed it back to her lawyer, asking if he would be kind enough to return the package to her. Wow, she knew exactly how to infuriate me and this time she really struck a chord.

At the beginning of March I tried to arrange another meeting with Mark. His birthday is at the end of March and we wanted to be able to celebrate it with him and give him his presents. My daughter, Kerrie, wasn't available at this time, so I was thankful when a friend of mine offered her place for us to meet for the day. Carla agreed we could have a visit with him for a few hours on the day after his birthday. It dawned on me that this would be the perfect opportunity to arrange to have the second assessment done. I then contacted my lawyer who put me in touch with a Government Certified Assessment Officer, and plans were made to meet with Christine Malone on March 26 at 12:00. I considered telling Carla about the assessment but decided not to, knowing she would never allow it to happen if I did.

As agreed, Carla dropped Mark off at half past twelve, giving Christine time to do the assessment and leave before everyone began arriving for the party at 1 pm. It was a small intimate party with only the immediate family and close friends invited and as we sat around the table just before the cake was brought out, Mark brought our attention to the new phone Carla had just bought for him. After taking a closer look we noticed it wasn't a phone at all. It was a taping device! Unbeknown to Mark we turned it off knowing Carla was the one who put him up to this stunt. Everyone was shocked to think she would send Mark for a visit to spy on us. By now I was beyond the point of being surprised and well aware of how this was a prime example of Carla using Mark by taking advantage of his naivety to get what she wanted.

At five o'clock the following morning all hell broke loose when Carla woke up Mark's worker ranting about the assessment and wanting to know how they could have allowed this to happen? In return, I received an e-mail, from them, chastising me for going behind Carla's back to have the assessment done. I answered back telling them I didn't feel I owed Carla an explanation about anything I did with Mark and reminded them nothing had been settled legally in regards to guardianship of him. Carla had obviously listened to the tape of our visit and although legally she didn't have exclusive rights to Mark, she did have physical possession of him. From that point on, in spite of our constant requests to see him she held him hostage and refused to allow him to leave her property to visit with us.

With a renewed sense of urgency we found ourselves caught up in the business of trying to receive guardianship of Mark as Carla continued to make it almost impossible for us to have a relationship with him. Her unrelenting capers, designed to humiliate and demoralize, only proved to strengthen our quest to bring Mark back to his family. I had always hoped Carla would prove me wrong in my opinion of her but she never did. There was always another underhanded deed to contend with and she clearly showed no intentions of allowing us to have a meaningful relationship with Mark. I'd witnessed the greed in her and had observed evidence of her constant deceitfulness. At this point I found myself completely obsessed with eliminating Carla from our lives and protecting Mark from her.

One day, in the midst of all the insanity surrounding our dealings with the lawyers I was surprised to receive a call from Robert. I hadn't heard from him since before Sarah passed away.

"Hi Robert, how are you? It's so good to hear from you! Where are you staying? We've been trying to get in touch with you!" I exclaimed.

"Oh, I've been around and thought it was about time I contacted you." He said, "I heard you are going for guardianship of Mark. Knowing firsthand how evil that woman can be, Mark needs to come out of there and I just want to say if there's anything I can do to help just let me know."

"Thanks Robert. I appreciate that. I agree with you about Mark and if I think of anything I'll be in touch." I replied. Then I asked, "I need to ask you something that's been bothering me for a long time."

Go ahead!" He said.

"Right after Sarah's memorial Carla said we needed to go to the house to collect anything of hers we wanted to take back with us. She said when you heard of her death you would change the locks and not let anyone in to get anything. Is that true?"

"Of course not!" He exclaimed. "Man, she's something else! Let me tell you a few things about Carla. The morning after the accident I still hadn't heard anything about it. I was filling up with gas and Carla drove right past me smiling and waving. She didn't even stop to tell me what had happened to Sarah the day before. It was such a heartless thing to do. I'll never forgive her for that and as far as me changing the locks on the house I didn't even have a key to get into the house myself. Carla was the only one with a key and warned me to stay away from there. She wouldn't even let me in there to get my own stuff out. Remember? I was court ordered to stay away when Sarah and I split up. I wasn't allowed to have any access to the house."

Come to think of it I did recall Carla locking the door when we left the house that day.

Then Robert went on to say, "The day Sarah was killed the final papers were drawn up to allow her to take possession of the house and all that remained, to finalize the agreement, was my signature. Immediately after Sarah's death Carla went to court to have them rule that, as the executor of Sarah's estate, she be allowed to continue with the proceedings on Sarah's behalf. By that time I wasn't sure if I wanted to let the house go or not, so I was looking into how I could hold onto it. That's when I started to notice Carla following me. It seemed like every time I went somewhere she would be parked out front, across the road or somewhere nearby where I could see her. She gave me the creeps and I started to leave places through the back door so she wouldn't be able to follow me. I was renting a room at the time and when I came home one day she was waiting out front for me. When she saw me she hopped out of the truck and pounced on me before I could get to the front door. She started shouting, "When are you going to sign those papers!" I told her I didn't want to speak to her and asked her to leave. I went inside the lobby and next thing I knew she was right in my face hollering "If you know what's good for you, you'll sign those papers!" To tell you quite honestly I'm frightened of her and it's not just her that scares me, even though she is evil, it's the people she associates with who are capable of causing me great bodily harm."

"Oh, my God, Robert, what are you going to do? " I asked in disbelief.

"I'm probably going to sign off before they find me in a ditch someday. It's just not worth it to have her involved in my life." He sighed.

When we hung up I sat for quite a while going over our conversation in my mind and realized more than ever how important it was to get Mark away from her.

Both government assessments deemed Mark incapable of managing his own affairs and our affidavit for guardianship of him was submitted to the courts. Things seemed to be moving along nicely although we were still trying to have an original death certificate sent to the financial advisor from

Carla so he could amend Mark's trust fund. Repeated attempts to gain an original certificate had failed. In fact, when our lawyer's office continued to enquire about having a copy sent out to them, so they could finalize the trust, they were told to stop harassing Carla. Finally, after five months of trying to no avail the public guardian and trustee was contacted. They intervened and eventually managed to get Carla's lawyer to comply with our request.

It had been a very long, cold winter for us that year and by the time spring arrived we were feeling trapped in the mire of Carla's endless wrath. It seemed no matter how we tried it was impossible to get ahead of her taunting endeavors to prolong the guardianship procedure. Doug and me were anxiously waiting and more than ready to start taking advantage of the change in seasons. Being free to breathe in the fresh spring air, revel in the warmth of the sunshine and busy ourselves in natures budding beauty was a refreshing deterrent. Returning to enjoying our morning coffee on the back deck overlooking the swelling of the river and observing the return of the songbirds, gave a whole new meaning to the start of the day.

Previously, I'd been authorized to sign for Mark's funding. April was the beginning of the fiscal year for WAFRS, so they called to ask me to consider continuing authorizing Mark's funding. This meant I would be responsible for authorizing any invoices submitted by Carla. My first thought was to refuse to give her any money at all but on second thought I realized it would only be punishing Mark if she didn't receive enough money to meet his needs. Besides, if the money isn't used there's a chance the funding would be cut off. After looking into what the average caregiver received as payment, in her area, I learned two hundred and fifty dollars a week was a fair wage. As much as it pained me to see Carla receive any compensation at all I reluctantly called them to authorize one thousand dollars a month to be paid to Carla out of Mark's individualized funding. If she required more to cover Mark's expenses she would have to submit a request for it to me.

This was a far cry from what Sarah was handing over to her. Sarah fought for years to ensure Mark would have the maximum government funding at his disposal, so on top of the thirteen thousand dollars Mark received annually from O.D.S.P., there was close to another twenty-five thousand dollars available to him through specialized government funding for a total of thirty-eight thousand dollars annually. Previously, Sarah was making sure Carla received the entire amount for Mark's care.

Now that I had been given the responsibility of authorizing all payments coming from Mark's funding I familiarized myself with the guidelines of dispersing the funds. I was determined to respect my newly appointed position by assuring the money was used wisely. I know Sarah funneled all of Mark's funding directly through to Matt and Carla allowing them free reign over the use of it. As I'd suspected many of Carla's family and friends ended up on the payroll, making it impossible to know if anyone was actually working on Mark's behalf or not. Regardless, I saw this as an unhealthy situation because Mark now remained totally isolated within Carla's personal circle of friends and family. My intentions were to break through the controlled lifestyle Mark was living and I hoped to hire skilled caregivers to get him involved in the community. Although I wasn't personally involved with Mark at that time I felt it was necessary for him to experience life beyond Carla.

~ Chapter Twelve ~

*"Oh, what a tangled web we weave,
when at first we practice to deceive."
~ Sir Walter Scott*

When it came to Mark, it was clear Carla and I had our own agenda for wanting guardianship. My focus was on bringing Mark back home to his family and saw no reason why that wasn't possible. After all, I am his only living sibling. I am his blood sister. His entire life I cared and looked out for him, always keeping his best interests at heart. On the other hand, I believe from years of observing Carla's behavior, her intentions in caring for Mark were based on her own selfish needs. Her reason for being in charge of him has had little to do with Mark's wellbeing and more to do with her being in the position to take advantage of him. The mania Carla exhibited, time and time again, in making sure Mark was under her control bordered on insanity. Witnessing her obscene behavior only motivated me to prepare for a fight to the finish to bring him back to us.

I knew if Carla had her wish she would eliminate me entirely from Mark's life. I was a thorn in her side and the only person standing in the way of her pulling off the perfect scam. Without me in the picture she would be free to take advantage of my sister's entire estate and be in complete control of Mark's trust and his government funding. Because of my awareness of her deluded manipulation of the situation, the idea of him being under her control haunted me. Being no match for her evil ways left me at a great disadvantage. I was fully aware of what she was capable of and I was fully aware of Mark's vulnerability. She had complete control of him, 24/7, mind, body and soul and I anguished over the harm she could do to him. Now, more than ever, it was essential to keep moving forward with receiving guardianship of my brother, it was the only way I knew of bringing him back into the fold.

At this point, Doug and I were fully engaged in the whole Carla scenario. Our every waking thought revolved around gaining access to Mark and our conversations focused entirely on her. We had never come across the likes of this woman and spent endless hours trying to figure out the rhyme or reason for her outlandish behavior. One evening, while having a discussion about Carla's shoplifting conviction we decided to punch her name into the computer. Not knowing what to expect we were surprised to find her name on a list attached to an article reported on June 6, 2006 and it was published in her local newspaper. Entitled *"Woman Banned From Wal-mart Stores for Stealing"*, we just couldn't believe our eyes! We immediately contacted the newspaper to find out if they would be able to mail the article to us. Being an older write up, we were told it had been sent to the archives at the Port Elgin library. When we contacted the library they agreed to send us a copy. We were ecstatic!

We had no idea what information would be contained in the article. At best, we were hoping for a few lines mentioning Carla's name and the conviction handed out to her, so you can imagine how amazed we were when a week later we received the write up and saw it was a half page article, reporting every single detail brought out in court that day. Apparently, a security guard followed Carla around the store and watched as she pulled plastic Wal-mart bags from her purse, filled them with food and clothing, then placed them in Mark's shopping cart. When Mark's cart was full they proceeded to the front of the store. Once the opportune time presented itself she prompted Mark to leave the store without paying for the merchandise. Carla pled not guilty to the charges and tried to pass off mis-dated, phony receipts in her defense but video cameras had caught her in the act and the judge didn't believe a word she said. She was found guilty of the charges, banned from all Wal-mart stores for life plus she was given five years probation. I have to admit I let out a chuckle once I realized, after all this time we finally had proof of Carla's guilt and more importantly Mark's innocence. Our suspicions had been verified and we were now able to lay our doubts to rest.

My thoughts immediately turned to Sarah. I was left thinking what a shame it was that she put so much trust in Carla. Because of Carla's inability to admit the truth Sarah died believing Mark was responsible for stealing from Wal-mart. After finding the newspaper article and positive proof of Carla's guilt, exonerating Mark from any connection to her criminal activity, I realized the extent of this woman's ruthlessness. It made clear how Carla was able to manipulate and control Mark to her advantage. The mere fact she allowed him to take the blame for her wrong-doing and had Sarah convinced he needed to pay for her legal fees and her pardon to have her record erased made me wonder what else she used and blamed him for. I will never understand how Carla managed to pull the wool over Sarah's eyes all those years and was left wondering if Sarah ever set Carla straight on the truth in her final days, leading up to her fatal demise.

We barely had a chance to digest the damning information contained in the newspaper article when a letter arrived from the public guardian and trustee. It was a copy of a letter sent to Carla informing her they had finished doing an audit on Mark's finances and were advising her that Sarah's estate had been put on notice. They were considering putting a claim against Mark's trust for substantial withdrawals of forty-five thousand and twenty-five thousand dollars. I was left speechless as I thought back to the day we met with WAFRS and we were told how Carla was enquiring about twenty-five thousand dollars that was supposed to be in Sarah's account when she passed away. I had no idea why this money was in

Sarah's account and I certainly didn't know anything about why forty-five thousand dollars had been moved out of Mark's trust. I could only speculate a good portion of it went towards paying Carla's legal fees and pardon and the rest went into Carla's pocket.

WAFRS had been a great source of support for us throughout this entire time and as a result there were many meetings. During one of our meetings someone asked if Mark was registered for the Cumberland class action. This was the first time we had ever heard of a class action involving him. When we enquired we found that litigation had been brought against Cumberland Regional Center for alleged allegations of abuse to the residents. They were seeking a settlement of two billion dollars.

Since the doors opened in 1876 residents at Cumberland had been ruthlessly abused, physically, sexually and emotionally, by the staff. I remembered a letter my mom showed me years ago before she passed it on to my sister. It stated as a child Mark had been sexually assaulted by an attendant when he was a resident at Cumberland. Because Carla had access to all my sister's papers she would be in possession of the letter now. That letter would qualify Carla to apply, on Mark's behalf, for financial compensation from the class action.

Thinking back to Mark's time spent at Cumberland I could only imagine what else he was subjected to and I found myself haunted by his cries and pleas to go home with us when we'd visit him each month. My heart broke for him. I've always found it hard to believe there are people out there who are capable of taking advantage of others who are so helpless and vulnerable. If the class action was won Mark would receive quite a sizable amount of money. This would be great for Mark but I saw it as a very powerful incentive for Carla to go to the extremes she has in order to keep him under her control. I proceeded to look into the pending litigation and was told Mark was already represented in the claim.

Contact with Mark became increasingly difficult after our visit with him for his birthday. Understandably, Carla took offence at our ploy to have Mark assessed without her knowledge but in our defense we were left with no other choice. From that point on she monitored and controlled every phone call we made to him and repeatedly cancelled out on any arrangements that were made to visit him at his trailer. Sadly, there was absolutely nothing we could do about it. We were at her mercy and she knew it. Each time we talked Mark would ask me where his money is and accuse me of spending it. No matter how many times I told him I had no access to his money he would get very angry with me and insist I did. Our phone calls to each other became strained and it was disheartening when I began hearing someone in the background coaching Mark to repeat rude and mean comments.

There was this one call, in particular, that stands out in my mind. I called Mark one morning just to say hello. He answered and it was clear by his voice he was excited to hear from me. Almost immediately,

I heard someone in the background say "tell her she's an idiot!" Mark then proceeded to call me an idiot. I know he wasn't capable of realizing the implications of what he'd said. He was only doing what he was told but I felt it necessary to point out to him how wrong that was to say such a hurtful thing. Mark had no idea he was being manipulated and over time because of the lies Carla found necessary to drill into his head about me, it became impossible to have any kind of conversation with him. Knowing he was totally under the control of Carla I feared losing touch with him completely. I could hear by the tone of his voice he was beginning to change. Around that time, I started to notice an unmistakable sense of meanness beginning to peek through. Sadly, the Mark I'd come to know and love began to fade away. He seemed to have lost his innocence.

During our limited conversations Mark would express how impressed he was with all the gifts Carla was showering on him, reiterating time and time again, that Carla was his "Guardian Angel" and he wouldn't be seeing us until after court. Then, for whatever reason Carla sent an email to say she would allow us to have a private visit with Mark in his trailer after June 23 and if we wanted we could have access to his pool that day. So arrangements were made to visit with him. We were so excited to finally be able to see him, even though Carla only allowed us a span of three hours to visit. Mark was equally excited and asked us to invite all of his nieces and nephews to join us for the pool party. Carla said she had recently installed a large pool, as well as, an eight person hot tub with all the bells and whistles in the backyard for Mark. Her generous gifts brought mounds of praise from Mark and he couldn't wait to show us his new toys. I sat in disbelief of Carla's incredulous cunning. Of course Mark would receive the benefits of her generosity but let's not kid ourselves it was also another perk for her and her family. Assuming everything was purchased on Mark's dime I found it hard to join in on his exuberance.

The weather was incredibly hot that day, so, by the time we arrived at the trailer the kids all jumped into the pool to cool down while Mark remained inside the trailer talking with Doug and me. After looking around I noticed there was a surveillance camera hooked up in the corner of the living room. Although I knew it had been installed for Carla to be able to keep an eye on Mark, it gave me the creeps to think of her up at the house watching and listening to every word we said. Immediately we disconnected it. Our focus that day was on enjoying the little time we had with Mark but trying to have a pleasant conversation with him turned out to be futile. He was fixated on knowing what I had done with his money and constantly made the point that he would not be coming to visit us until after court. Getting him off the topic of court and money was a near impossibility and as such everything escalated very quickly and soon became very intense. It was clear, by his unmerited show of anger someone was filling his mind with untruths about us. I had no idea what to do about this unexpected situation but I did know as long as he was left under her control, things would only get worse.

After we'd been there for half an hour I noticed Matt on the back deck firing up his brand new, larger than life BBQ. Five minutes later Carla came out and pranced around the pool in her flowing black lace cover up and her silver, pom-pom embellished mules. Soon their friends showed up with their kids bearing coolers and salads. It was plain to see they were there for a preplanned poolside party. Shortly afterwards, all of our kids came in from outside saying they were asked to leave the pool area. I was so mad I couldn't think straight. This was supposed to be our time together with Mark. Carla had promised us our privacy and the use of the pool for the afternoon and here we were, all crammed into a stifling hot trailer for the remainder of our visit. I couldn't help but wonder if this impromptu gathering of Carla's friends wasn't in retaliation of us disconnecting the surveillance camera and what about Mark? Didn't she see how disappointed he was that the pool party with his family was suddenly shut down?

Positioning herself on a deck chair, in plain sight of Mark, Carla began motioning for him to come and sit with her. When Mark noticed her he began to go towards the door but before he could open it I managed to blurt out,

"If you go away and leave us here alone we will have no choice but to leave and go home right now! Is that what you want?"

Immediately, Mark sat down and turned his back to the window ignoring her inviting gestures. It was hot and it was crowded but we made the best of it and the remainder of our visit turned out to be pretty enjoyable. Time passed quickly and it was now five o'clock. Our visit had come to an end and we were all sad knowing it was time for us to leave but as we were saying our goodbyes, I noticed Carla barreling down the back yard towards the trailer, black lace flying in the wind and silver mules digging into the dirt. When we opened the door to find out what she wanted, she hollered out,

"It's five o'clock and your visit is over. It's time for you to leave, now!"

Then, turning around abruptly she went back to join all her buddies by the poolside. It was obvious her show of aggression towards us was for the benefit of her friends sitting there watching but it left me physically shaken and emotionally stunned. This was our first visit in three and a half months and Carla intentionally sabotaged our time together, every step of the way. All we asked for was a little privacy and she didn't even have the decency to let us have that. This unnecessary exhibit of control further proved to me we were dealing with a very sick, demented woman who couldn't get past her own animosity to realize she was really only hurting Mark. Mark loves his family and it was plain to see he was left confused by Carla's spitefulness. We quickly gathered our things and left. As we drove off I found myself teary-eyed wondering if I would ever have a relationship with my brother again. Then, I remembered Carla gesturing for him to join her by the pool and him turning his back on her, choosing to stay with us. That brief moment of defiance showed me he really did care and I was left with a glimmer of hope as we pulled out of the driveway.

Before we began our trip to visit Mark we were contacted by a police officer, stationed in the Port Elgin area. She asked if we would drop in to the station before starting our trip back home after the pool party. Apparently, WAFRS had reported a number of allegations presented to them by some people who were concerned about Mark's situation. These allegations all had to do with varying degrees of abuse and misconduct by Carla and her family members towards Mark. Curious to find out what this was all about we dropped the kids off at Kerrie's place then returned to the police station in Port Elgin. After we were finally seated the officer came into the office, sat down behind her desk and began to explain to us,

"I am sorry to hear about what you have been dealing with but I've looked into the allegations against Carla and although what she has done is morally wrong, she has done nothing criminal that she could be charged with and I feel if we went snooping around her place and got involved in her business she may just close the door on everyone and completely isolate Mark. I've dealt with her kind before and this type of person is very difficult to nail down, so as long as WAFRS is keeping an eye on things you're probably best to let them be your eyes and ears."

Her answer indicated to us she knew exactly what kind of personality we were dealing with, so we took the opportunity to delve into Carla's disturbing behavior and the suspicions we had regarding Sarah's death. We attempted to get her to see our desperation but she seemed unfazed. She went back to her computer and pulled up the reports having to do with Sarah's accident. After taking a moment to look things over she turned to us and merely said,

"The file concerning your sister's accident has been closed and will not be reopened. The investigation is closed and there's nothing more I can do for you. You may as well go home and try to get on with your lives."

We walked out of there that night no further ahead than when we walked in. That was the second time we had been told the investigation of Sarah's accident was closed and would not be reopened. We just couldn't understand why no one felt the overwhelming incriminating information we had wasn't worth looking into. We returned home that evening confused and wondering how one person could do so much damage to a family and not be held accountable for their actions. It just didn't seem right how she could continually defy the law and get away with it. Disappointed, we were left with no choice but to try to get on with our lives. Everything we had witnessed and knew for a fact about Carla lay heavy on our heads. As a result, we felt compelled to share our story with everyone and anyone who would listen to what we had to say, hoping someone might have an answer to our questions. Baffled and at a complete loss to know where to turn to next, we were left asking ourselves "Where do we go from here to find justice?"

A short time later Pastor Barry, from one of the churches in our town, happened to be driving past our place and stopped to admire our latest purchase, a sweet little 1952 MG. We were busy shining her up to get ready to enter a car show on the week end. As we engaged in having an enjoyable conversation with the pastor he happened to mention, at one time, he worked as an editor, broadcaster and journalist for a newspaper near Port Elgin, not far from where my sister lived in Hampton. As soon as he mentioned this to us we thought there may be a possible lead here and began sharing our story about Sarah's accident and Mark's abduction with him. We thought he might be able to put us in touch with someone who would be willing to look into further investigating the circumstances leading up to and surrounding the accident. We were desperate and open to anything that could possibly lead us to expose Carla's true character. The pastor left that day promising to look into things for us and we were left with the hope that we would possibly see justice after all. A week later, the pastor returned to inform us there was nothing he could do to help us. Unfortunately, we were left to continue obsessing over Carla. But we still kept our eyes and ears open. We were keen on accepting any possible lead that would help us to incriminate her.

One morning, shortly after our encounter with the pastor, I opened my emails to find a message from Respite. I found a copy of two receipts, totaling twenty-four hundred dollars, to be reimbursed to Carla out of Mark's funding, along with a request, from her, they be paid as soon as possible. Before authorizing payment I took a few moments to glance over the receipts. The first receipt, in the amount of one thousand dollars was to cover Mark for two weeks at summer camp. I didn't have a problem with approving this payment except I knew he wasn't at camp for the two weeks specified. First of all, I knew this because our latest visit with him fell right in the middle of the time given on the receipts and secondly I found it strange that the receipt was made out and signed by someone I knew to be one of Carla's friends.

The second receipt in the form of a sales slip was for the amount of fourteen hundred and sixty four dollars to cover campground fees for a weekend spent at Seven Hills Country Jamboree. I knew Carla attended the Jamboree every year and had taken Mark with her a number of times. I also knew they camped when they attended this weekend but I felt the amount on the sales slip seemed a little high for two people for three days. Even though Mark's funding would cover these charges allowing him to have one other person attend with him, something just didn't seem right. I called the Jamboree to find out what their rates were and found out the amount on the sales slip covered four people to camp for the weekend, not two. Now I understood why she submitted the nonspecific sales slip and not the actual receipt that would have stated exactly how many people were covered in the price.

I held off on authorizing payment until I called WAFRS to inform them of my discovery, explaining to them why I couldn't approve payment for either of the amounts. They agreed with my decision and left it up to me to let Carla know. I felt it was only right to give her a chance to explain the discrepancies I had discovered, so I sent her an email pointing out my concerns and asked if she would clarify the details. Immediately I received a message back from her saying she didn't need to explain any of Mark's activities and asked me to return the receipts to her. I made copies of the receipts and promptly returned them as requested. I doubt Carla was aware that I was now the one authorizing payments from Mark's funding. She just figured it was business as usual and got caught in the act. I was left wondering about how many fraudulent receipts Carla had actually submitted and been paid for over the years?

A few weeks later Doug and me were getting ready to begin our day when the phone rang. It was Pastor Barry asking if he could come over to see us that morning. We asked if he'd like to come right away and he accepted our invitation. Within minutes he was at the door. We could see he was visibly shaken and after we were all settled around the table with a fresh cup of coffee he began by asking,

"Did you two set me up?"

Doug and I looked at each other totally confused as the pastor emphasized,

"Did ...you ... two ... set... me... up?"

"We have no idea of what you are talking about but to answer your question, no, we did not set you up. What is this all about?" Doug enquired.

The pastor began to explain that he was having coffee with a friend in town at Tim Horton's last week when a young fellow who was sitting at the table beside them joined in on their conversation. When the pastor's friend left, the young fellow who introduced himself as Dale moved over to the pastor's table, so they could continue with the conversation they were having.

Somehow, the conversation led to Dale confessing to something that had bothered him for some time. Dale told the pastor that he'd met with a friend last Halloween night. His friend asked if he'd like to go for a drive with him. They were travelling north-east of Port Elgin when they came up to a woman driving an SUV. His friend began to speed up and continued to follow the SUV with his high beams turned on, forcing her to speed even faster until she lost control of her vehicle and ran off the road ending up in a farmer's field. They didn't stop to see what happened to the woman and from that point on he had a hard time living with the fact they just drove off not knowing the fate of the woman behind the wheel. After listening to the young man's confession the pastor realized it was the burden of guilt that must have plagued Dale all these months. He told him, to ease his conscience, to go to the police and tell them his story. Shortly afterwards Dale got up, excused himself, then left.

By the time the pastor arrived home he began to realize the similarities between what he had just heard from Dale and the information we shared with him about Sarah's accident. He struggled for days with the idea of ministerial confidentiality but eventually put in a call to our local police department. After being shuffled around to different area departments he was finally put in touch with the department that dealt with my sister's accident. The pastor was told the only accident on that particular night that even came close to the information he'd passed on to them was my sister's accident. Then, the pastor was informed by the officer, "I hope you realize what you have just told me takes this accident to a whole different level of murder". The pastor suggested the officer speak to Doug and me and gave him our number. Oddly, we never received a call from the police.

When the pastor finished speaking we were dumbfounded. It was hard to comprehend what we'd just heard but now we understood why the pastor might think we'd set him up. The whole scenario at Timmy's was almost too bizarre to be true. While we finished our coffee we continued to try to make sense of the latest information shared by the pastor and what it all meant. We were left asking ourselves, *how is it possible for Dale to walk into a Timmy's so far from his hometown and choose to confess to a pastor that was familiar with the story of my sister's accident?* We had no other explanation except to conclude it was an act of providence. Nothing else could explain the whys or hows of what had taken place and our hopes were lifted because if this was, in fact, an act of providence there could only be a divine ending.

Just because a whole new scenario and fresh characters had been thrown into the mix didn't mean I'd been thrown off Carla's trail. It only proved to confirm my thoughts of Carla having something to do with my sister's death. Carla never did do her own dirty work. She always had someone else do it for her. Whether it be using Mark to steal for her or having someone else to abduct Mark from us. It wasn't too much of a stretch to think she would get someone else to run Sarah off the road. After all, Sarah did tell Doug, only weeks before her accident, she was concerned about someone following her a number of times with their high beams on, when she was driving home from Carla's at night. Coincidence? I think not!

One morning, over coffee, Doug happened to ask, "Have you read the article written about the woman who was scammed by her caregiver yet?"

"No, I haven't. It must be good if you're mentioning it to me. What's it all about?" I asked.

"Well, there's this elderly woman, a senior, who hired a live-in caregiver to take care of her so she could remain in her home. The caregiver moved in with her and over the course of a few months, with the help of a low-life lawyer and a sleazy real estate agent, managed to swindle the old woman out of everything she was worth. It's kind of interesting how similar the story was with what we're going through with Mark right now. You should read it for yourself." He said.

"Sounds like an interesting article. I'll do that." I answered, as I took my last sip.

I sat down at the computer and pulled up the article Doug suggested to read. It was uncanny how similar the scenario was to what we were experiencing. Although the circumstances were different the scam was the same. After befriending an elderly woman, a live-in care giver then proceeded to con the woman by taking advantage of her vulnerability and trust. Before long the old woman had signed everything she had over to the care giver, house, bank accounts and all. Crazy thing is there was nothing illegal about what was done to this poor woman. Everything would have stopped there except through a strange course of events, the old woman's unfortunate circumstances made its way onto Dick Branson's desk, a top notch reporter who thankfully saw the injustice of it all and pushed for the case to be brought before the courts. The courts were able to see the injustice and fortunately everything was returned to the old woman. *Wow, maybe there is such a thing as justice after all!* I thought to myself.

I was impressed with the article, so without hesitation, I sent off a comment to Branson's email, congratulating him on a job well done. To qualify my empathy with his article I gave a few details of the situation regarding Mark and Carla. Within minutes

I received a message back from him saying he would like to speak to me and asked if I would give him a call. I really didn't expect to hear back from the reporter and I couldn't wait to tell Doug what had just evolved. After discussing whether I should get back to him or not we finally agreed this could be the break we were waiting for to get to the bottom of Carla's impervious deeds. After all, the police didn't see the obvious mockery or miscarriage of justice in any of Carla's deception and we thought maybe this could possibly be a way of bringing Mark back to us. We had no idea where this would lead to but we felt it certainly couldn't hurt to try.

I felt right at ease speaking with Dick as I tried to fill him in on the details. Clearly, my story could be divided into two very distinct areas of contention. The first area dealing with Carla's behavior from the time she was introduced into my family's lives up to the time of my sister's death and the second involves everything to do with Carla from the time of Sarah's death to the present. Rehashing either area would have produced quite a compelling story but the reporter's intentions were to bring light onto the fact two people, a sister and a care giver, were vying for guardianship of Mark, an elderly handicapped man, so I restricted my facts to our plight of obtaining guardianship of Mark. We'd been speaking on a regular basis for a couple of weeks when Dick informed me he would be travelling to speak with Carla and Mark to get their side of the story. I had tried my best to present everything as truthful as

I could but knowing Carla the way I did, I was left feeling very uneasy about him talking to her.

Upon his return, Dick called to tell me what he'd come up with. My heart was racing as I sat and paid close attention to what he had to say.

"When I arrived, Mark was walking outside in the yard with Montana, his pet pot belly pig and was all smiles when he saw me. After introducing himself to me he invited me into the house to meet Carla. We sat for some time talking when Carla asked if I would like to see Mark's room. I tell you, it was picture perfect with sports posters all over the walls and teddy bears propped on the bed. You really couldn't ask anything more for him. At that point we went back downstairs and continued our discussion. Then, sitting there like a proud peacock, she pulled out a paper dated June 23 and showed it to me. When I read it I realized it was a legal document appointing her as Mark's power of attorney. It looks as though she....."

I abruptly broke in, "Hold on a minute. Did you just say she has legal papers stating she's been appointed power of attorney for Mark? Oh, my God! I can't believe this! How is that even possible?" I blurted out behind my tears. "That means it's all over. There's no point anymore. She found a way to do the impossible." I managed to utter before I completely broke down.

Not really understanding the full significance of what he just told me, the reporter did his best to ease my unhinged reaction but I was so shaken I found I wasn't able to continue with our conversation, so I hung up. Once I managed to get myself settled down enough to start thinking straight, my first thoughts were to call the lawyer and fill him in on the latest twist.

I just couldn't believe she was able to do what she'd done and neither could the lawyer. How it is even possible after we had two certified assessment officers attest to the fact Mark was not capable of making that decision. Besides, the law clearly states; neither a caregiver or a landlord can be appointed power of attorney and Carla was both. My lawyer, dumbfounded by this latest course of events, suggested we meet to come up with another plan of action.

A letter was sent out to Carla's lawyer requesting proof of her legal appointment in light of the fact two assessments had already been done stating he was incapable of appointing a power of attorney for himself. Within a short while we received a 'Letter of Opinion' endorsed by a psychologist, affiliated with York University, who was hired by Carla to do a third assessment to conclude Mark was capable of appointing a power of attorney. A legal document dated June 23 had been drawn up by a lawyer, stating Mark had appointed Carla as his power of attorney accompanied the statement.

The letter of opinion began by pointing out the criteria for a person having the capacity to grant a power of attorney for personal care.

A person is capable of giving a power of attorney for personal care if the person,

a. Has the ability to understand whether the proposed power of attorney has a genuine concern for the person's welfare
b. Appreciates that the person may need to have the proposed attorney make decisions for the person.

Of which Mark has neither.

The letter of opinion, written by the well-versed psychologist, stated that although Mark did not know his address, did not know how to make a ham sandwich, was not able to grasp abstract ideas, did not know how to use a telephone and did not verbalize sentences well enough to be understood, she felt he was able to appoint a power of attorney for himself. Except for the letter expressing that Mark repeatedly stated Carla was his "guardian angel and he wanted his guardian angel to take care of him" the document was very similar to the two assessments we had done stating Mark was not capable of appointing power of attorney.

Reading through the misguided opinions of the doctor and Mark's comments only proved to me he had been coached to say exactly what Carla wanted him to say. The control Carla had over the whole situation was obvious to anyone who was familiar with the entire scenario. Unfortunately the unsuspecting doctor had no idea of who she was dealing with and fell for her premeditated scheme. After reading the assessment I was appalled and remained in disbelief.

My lawyer, completely baffled by this latest twist, suggested we continue with our application for guardianship and contest the doctor's Statement of Opinion. Carla's power of attorney gave her the legal right to make all personal care decisions for Mark. We had no choice but to try and discredit the doctor. Obviously Carla failed to inform her of the pending battle going on for guardianship of Mark and I can only imagine the woeful story that was presented to the unsuspecting doctor. The story of a poor caregiver whose employer had been killed in a tragic car accident, leaving an elderly handicapped man for her to care for. What a saint!

As I continued on with all the legalities I could feel the divide, between me and my brother, widen. Here we were back at square one, facing the fact that Carla had found a way to win the case against all odds and end up in charge of my brother. The thought of her having complete control of Mark and how she would use him for everything he is worth was almost more than I could bear.

After receiving the approval of the doctor, Carla would have taken Mark along with the ill-gotten statement to a lawyer who would have had to agree Mark was capable of appointing Carla as his power of attorney. Any lawyer has the right to draw up the papers for power of attorney after they have concluded the appointee is of sound mind to consent. The papers are signed in the privacy and absolute confidentiality of a lawyer's office. Once the papers are signed that's it, it's done. Nothing has to be registered or reported, no background check or proof of relationship has to be investigated. There is nothing at all to hold anyone accountable. The system as it sits today beckons every type of deviant to take advantage of the vulnerable. It just isn't right!

Yes, Mark is capable of having strong feelings towards people and no doubt he cares for Carla in his own way, he is totally dependent on her but he is in no way capable of understanding the implications of appointing a power of attorney for himself. More importantly, I find it unbelievable this was allowed to happen right in the midst of a pending court case. I have no way of knowing what went on in that lawyer's office but I do know if the lawyer actually spoke to Mark, it would have been obvious he was not capable of appointing a power of attorney and there is no way a power of attorney would have been drawn up. At this point, as crazy as it sounds, I entertained the thoughts that maybe Matt sat in for Mark at the lawyer's office. Regardless, I was forced to accept Carla was now armed with the legal documents to give her the power to make all decisions on Mark's behalf.

Arriving home from the lawyer's office I walked through the front door feeling totally defeated and was considering the thoughts of walking away from it all. As I sat down with a cup of tea I started going through the mounds of paperwork we had accumulated throughout this whole ordeal. It was disheartening to think we had come this far only to have everything come to an abrupt stop. I picked up my sister's will and began reading it through in hopes of finding something that may help save Mark from Carla's clutches.

Instead, as I read through the sinfully vague document a paragraph popped out at me. It read in reference to Mark 'the amount thereof remaining shall be paid or transferred to him or her, or should such person die...while mentally incapable of managing property, to his or her legal personal representative.'

"Oh, my God!" I cried out. "Of course, this is why it was so important for her to become his power of attorney. If there's anything left of Mark's estate when he dies it will go to her."

I couldn't help but think what will happen to him when he becomes worth more to her dead than alive. Will he meet with the same demise as my sister? Here I was, once again, fearful for my brother being left at the mercy of such a corrupt human being and I realized I had to fight for him right to the bitter end.

Now that Carla had legal control of Mark I hoped she would feel secure enough to allow us to have some sort of relationship with him but she continued to see his family as a threat and was relentless in keeping him from us. One day I received a call from WAFRS. They thought I should know they had met with Carla to discuss allowing Mark to have regular visits with his niece, Kerrie, because they too were concerned about him being secluded in Carla's world and losing touch with his family. They suggested his niece be allowed to take Mark out for dinner once a month but Carla was strictly against him leaving her property without being chaperoned by someone of her choice. In fact, she was against Kerrie having any contact with him at all. Due to Carla's persistent ire the quest of Mark having any contact with his niece was dropped.

The first anniversary of Sarah's death was approaching and plans were made to meet with a few of her close friends and family at the roadside memorial. We tearfully gathered around the weathered wooden cross and after placing flowers and saying a heartfelt prayer we all went our separate ways. Some took a walk along the roadside reenacting the final moments of Sarah's life, some dared to venture into the adjacent field where Sarah took her last breath. I remained at the cross freshening it up as best I could by clearing away the abundance of unwanted weeds.

Lost in emotion I barely noticed a car approaching. It wasn't until the vehicle stopped and a woman rolled down the window and began talking that I was snapped back to reality and began to take note of what was happening around me. The unexpected intruder began to holler out,

"If I didn't know any better I'd think it was Sarah standing there. You must be her sister." She shouted.

"Yes, I am and you would be?" I asked.

"My name is Sharon; I was a good friend of Sarah's. It's terrible what happened to her and to think Carla ended up with Mark. I hear you're going for guardianship of him. I sure hope you get it. That Carla is something else. Sarah was such a sweetheart but it was a sin the way Carla treated her. She was so mean to her. I've seen her feed Sarah drinks until she passed out, then take the checkbook out of her purse and write a check for herself. I saw her take cash out of her purse too and the way she constantly made fun of her and laughed at her behind her back. That woman is ruthless. I really hope you manage to get Mark away from her. Well it was great meeting you. I have to run. Bye now."

Before I had a chance to say anything she sped off. I wasn't shocked by what I just heard, after all, it wasn't anything I hadn't heard before but it was clear Carla had played Sarah for a fool. It hurt to think my sister held Carla in such high esteem. I felt sick at heart but I took what this woman said as a clear sign for me not to give up and to keep fighting for Mark.

Once we were safe at home that evening I decided to open the mail and discovered a letter from the courts informing us of the court date for the guardianship hearing. It was nearing the end of November but the date was set for the following year on September 10. Almost eleven months away. It seemed like an eternity to have to wait for the final verdict of whether Mark would be coming home to us or not. We were already starting to prepare for Mark's return by purchasing a small house, situated close to our place, for him to live in. Mark's niece, Kerrie was planning to move to Fairport to care for him. We were excited to go to court and felt we'd come up with a great solution so Mark could return to his family and we reveled at the thought of finally ridding ourselves of Carla.

~ Chapter Thirteen ~

"The most important things in life aren't things."
~ Anonymous

The crisp autumn breeze blowing in through the bedroom window commanded me to get up out of bed early. Reaching the kitchen I discovered a note from Doug informing me he had already left to do some chores around town. After settling down behind the computer with my second cup of morning coffee I checked my calendar. Pleased to see there was nothing pressing to do on my list that day I let out a sigh of relief and sat back in my chair savoring the last sip of coffee. When the front door slammed shut I jumped as Doug came running into the office. Out of breath and shouting with excitement he dumped an armful of newspapers on the desk in front of me.

"It's in! It's in the paper today! The article's in! You won't believe it! It's the front page, feature article, colored pictures and all! Wait until you read it, you'll be impressed."

"Wow! This is exciting." I replied in anticipation. "Let me see one of those papers. I can't wait to see how it turned out."

He handed one of the papers to me and I quickly went into the kitchen to spread it out on the table. I was anxious to read what the reporter had to say after gathering information from Carla and me for over a month. After quickly glancing over the article I had to go over it a second time, taking care to digest and understand every single word that was written. After the second reading I tried summing everything up in my head. *I think it was good.* I thought to myself. *After all, he did quote me accurately and I did come off sounding as if I was somewhat intelligent and I think my interest in Mark's well-being came across as sincere. On the other hand, assuming he quoted Carla accurately, I felt her comments sounded a little foolish.* After pondering everything for a few moments I finally concluded. *"It really was a very in depth, well written article."* I sat back smiling and I was pleased.

Soon the phone was ringing off the hook with friends and family checking to see if we'd seen the paper yet, then just before noon Dick called to ask what I thought of it all.

"Wow! I had no idea this was going to be the feature article but all in all I think you did a pretty good job of portraying the gist of things. Good work!" I applauded him.

"What did you expect? I spent a good month putting it together. I'm rather pleased myself." He told me before adding, "I just got off the phone with Carla and she's not a happy camper at all. She's livid about me including some of her quotes and the fact I mentioned the theft charges."

"Well, to tell you the truth I thought you were going to lean more towards my side than you did but I understand you had to remain neutral and tell both sides. Whatever, it's out there now. I don't regret anything I said and I think you did a wonderful job of presenting the facts accurately."

The article was quite long and involved, so after we hung up I found it necessary to go back and read it thoroughly one more time. This time I wanted to focus on the highlights the reporter felt obliged to bring to light to make his story worthy of being a front page feature article. I began to read:

THE FIGHT FOR MARK

Mark is a child in a 57 year old body.
A death in his family has sparked a nasty battle for control of his long term care

He pointed out that when he travelled to Carla's, Mark seemed to be happy and oblivious to the nasty battle going on between us over his care. He then described Mark as a boy trapped in a man's body, followed by a short history of Mark's unfortunate circumstances surrounding his birth, resulting in him being mentally handicapped. Elaborating, he added Mark was sent to Cumberland Regional Centre in Barrie at the age of five. He then told about the two billion dollar class action with Mark being a possible recipient for his share of the settlement. He mentioned that Mark is in need of round the clock care and that Carla and I are fighting for guardianship of him. He points out that we both love and want what is best for Mark and we both claim the other is only after his money. We both deny the claim. Then, he points out how ironic it is that in a time when many with mental disabilities who require care have to wait decades before they receive a caregiver while Mark has two people willing to look after him.

Next, Branson set the stage by telling of the mistrust between Carla and I fueled by allegations of kidnapping, criminal wrongdoing, dueling mental capacity assessments and a questionable power of attorney. He pointed out that Mark carries a lot of financial benefits around with him. He receives $36,000.00 annually in government funding, as well as, being eligible for his portion of the billion dollar class action, once it is settled. Additionally, he is the heir of a hefty trust fund left by his mother. He added that I said Carla sees Mark as a "cash cow". Then, as I expected she would, Carla denied money as a motivation and claimed she wanted Mark with her because he is part of her family. *What a ridiculous statement! She is nothing more than a hired employee who I had actually fired at one point. She is not even remotely related!* I paused to shake my head at her foolish remark.

Next, Carla accused me of wanting to institutionalize Mark. *Another ridiculous statement!* I thought *if she knew what she was talking about she'd know all government run institutions were shut down years ago.* But, when she claimed Mark moved in with her permanently in 2004, I really started to burn. *That was an out and out lie!* I ranted to myself. *She's just trying to make herself look like more of a permanent fixture in Mark's life than she really is. Mark didn't move to Carla's until 2009 when a trailer was purchased for him to stay in at the far end of her property when my sister moved to Hampton.* Her twisted truth and constant stream of lies never ceased to amaze or upset me.

Carla told Dick she promised Sarah she would take care of Mark always and brought out a signed but undated note stating such. I'm assuming this was the same note she tried to pass off to the police the night she showed up at my door to try and take Mark away from us. The police didn't fall for it and personally I wouldn't put too much value on anything Carla says was signed by Sarah, after all, she didn't have a problem forging my name on the insurance documents and as I was told by a number of people, Carla was known to forge Sarah's checks.

Dick then went on to give a short summary of the facts surrounding Sarah's accident and pointed out that her will states that if any of the beneficiaries die "while mentally incapable of managing property, their share goes to his or her legal personal representative". The reporter must have found this to be an odd stipulation to be included in a will if he found it necessary to point it out in the article but then I personally found Sarah's entire will questionable.

He then quoted me as saying, "I not only lost my sister on October 31, 2011, but I also lost my brother."

Next, he pointed out the fact that one week after Sarah's death Carla travelled to Cambridge with Mark to cash in their life insurance claims. Adding, Carla took the unauthorized initiative to sign my name to the documents to have the money released. Carla claimed she had my permission to do so and she also claimed Mark's forty-seven thousand dollar portion was immediately sent to the Public Guardian and Trustee. This was also untrue. Mark's check was obtained on November 11 and she didn't hand the money over to the Public Guardian and Trustee until after I got them involved in mid-January to protect Mark's funds after Carla abducted him from us then they had to ask her to hand it over to them.

Branson then focused on Mark's abduction by pointing out that Mark was left with me while Carla went to China with a friend who was adopting a baby and after finding out Mark wanted to remain with me for awhile longer, Carla booked an immediate flight back home. After meeting with police then storming my house that evening, with the intentions of removing Mark, the police found it in Mark's best interest for him to remain with me. Then, Branson pointed out three weeks later, on January 8, Mark went missing while shopping at Wal-mart. A massive police search was done of the area and Mark eventually showed up at Carla's house, some 400 kms away. I called it kidnapping, Carla labeled it karma, saying "They should never have tried to take

Mark from us in the first place." I shook my head in disbelief of her twisted thinking.

He then goes on to mention the bizarre mental assessment initiated by Carla through a York University psychologist. 'A Letter of Opinion' emphasized what the psychologist concluded from Mark's answers to her questioning. She stated that although Mark was not capable of making a ham and cheese sandwich for himself, didn't know how to dial 911, couldn't tally up a pocketful of change and he said he would die if he didn't eat vegetables, she felt Mark was competent to give power of attorney to Carla for his personal care. When, the reporter asked for a statement from the psychologist and the lawyer responsible for writing up the power of attorney, neither were available for comment.

Branson then pointed out the law on power of attorney. The law is clear and states that anyone who is compensated for services or is the person's landlord cannot be power of attorney unless they are a relative. Carla claims she does control his monthly disability funds but Mark does not pay rent, only food. Then he states, in spite of the law Carla was appointed Mark's power of attorney.

Carla's 2006 conviction of theft is pointed out in detail to which she replies "I have never stolen a thing in my life. I know what happened. Mark knows what happened. Anyone who knows me knows the truth." Carla then says, "None of that matters, because I have since obtained a pardon allowing me to once again work with vulnerable people." After reading her statement I almost broke out laughing. *Unbelievable! Does she really think that explanation makes any sense? Does she even realize how foolish she sounds?*

Then, he went on to comment about Mark's room with all the Leaf's paraphernalia, toys and teddy bears and how happy Mark seemed to be. Even though it was difficult to understand what Mark was saying, when he was asked if he wanted to live with Robin he managed to say clearly, "No, not with Robin. It's too far. I live here." It saddened me to read what Mark said but after reminding myself of Mark's position, being totally reliant on Carla for his survival and Carla's complete control over him, I didn't take his comment to heart.

Carla commented on how difficult life with Mark is, especially with his bouts of anger. She went on to say she has suffered black eyes and swollen lips as a result of being punched and kicked by Mark. When asked why she keeps him she replied, "Because he's part of our family. I can't walk away as if I'm just hired help." Then, when Branson mentioned the property we purchased for Mark to live in after we receive guardianship, Carla replied, "Over my dead body. We're definitely going to challenge that. We love him like we would one of our own kids." *There she goes again claiming Mark is part of her family. She is and always has been Mark's caregiver. Mark is and always has been her client, nothing more than that!"* I affirmed to myself.

After reading the article in its entirety for the third time I once more took time to digest its content. I was overwhelmed and sick at heart that everything had come to this point. The fact our dirty laundry was being put on display for all the readers of a major newspaper to read was humiliating to me but obviously our situation was of public interest or the reporter wouldn't have been so thorough in his reporting and it wouldn't have been presented as a front page feature article.

All in all, I did get some sort of satisfaction knowing Carla's comments came off as sounding foolish but the truth of the matter was Carla was in control of Mark and there was nothing I could do about it. It was still ten months until our case was set to be heard in court and Mark was still being held hostage from his family. Carla made it very clear we were not to take him off her property and she had also made it clear any visits we had with him would be subject to her being present.

As Christmas approached we were hopeful that Carla would allow us to take Mark out for a family dinner. By this point, all contact between Carla and I plus any arrangements to do with Mark were made between our two lawyers. When she received our request, on December 12, to take Mark out for dinner at a local restaurant she promptly responded by saying Mark had a girlfriend named Dianne and she would only allow him to leave her property if he was accompanied by her. This was the first time we'd heard of Mark having a girlfriend and it seemed odd to me he'd never mentioned her name to us before this.

I had a funny feeling this was another one of Carla's stunts and I doubted Dianne was Mark's girlfriend at all. My gut feeling was that Dianne was someone Carla had lined up to accompany Mark and report back to her. If, in fact, Dianne was handicapped and a girlfriend of Mark's, I didn't want to be responsible for someone I didn't know if they had special needs. To avoid a bad situation I had the lawyer send another letter out to Carla asking to speak with Dianne's caregiver, in order to get some idea of what special care we needed to know about before committing to include Dianne in our visit. We received a letter back from Carla saying Dianne would not be accompanying Mark. I can only assume from this reaction Dianne did not have a caregiver, was not handicapped and was, in fact, someone Carla set up to spy on our time together.

Because Christmas was fast approaching, we immediately sent out another letter to let Carla know the arrangements we'd made for our day with Mark, confirming where to bring Mark for dinner and when to pick him up afterwards. Unfortunately, the lawyers left for Christmas break before we received a reply, leaving us with no alternative but to travel the 400 kilometers just in case Carla should decide to bring Mark, regardless of a reply. We had no way of knowing if Mark would show up or not and couldn't take the chance of him being disappointed. We made the long trip and waited three hours in the parking lot before we sadly began our journey back home, without seeing him.

I was furious with Carla for being so heartless. I was furious with the lawyers for not really caring enough to push matters along but most of all, I was furious with myself. Once again, I had allowed this woman to fool me into thinking she cared about anyone but herself. All I wanted to do was simply spend a few hours with my brother at Christmas and that was proving to be an impossible feat. I knew Carla had evil intentions when it came to Mark and I knew she was involved with him for her own self-serving reasons. She held Mark hostage in the confines of her own private little world and was not about to allow anyone, including his family, to penetrate the walls she had so meticulously built around him.

When we returned home I sent Carla an e-mail to let her know how angry I was with her for keeping us away from Mark, especially at Christmastime. A few minutes later I received a reply back from her stating that, "Well you didn't allow us to see Mark last year so why should we let you see him this year?" By this point I was tired of trying to make sense of her reasoning so I didn't even try but it was made perfectly clear we would not be seeing Mark anytime soon.

Surprisingly, the following day Mark called and it was obvious he was not aware of what we had just gone through to see him. We were having a pleasant conversation while I sat biding my time, waiting for the appropriate moment to cut in and bring up the subject of Dianne. To my surprise he began to refer to Dianne without me even having to ask. He prided himself in telling me Dianne was his girlfriend and boasted about being in love with her. He professed his love for her and told me how excited he was because he had just given her a beautiful diamond engagement ring for a Christmas present. When he invited Doug and me to their wedding in Carla's backyard in the spring, my heart sank as I questioned the possibility of marriage being a reality.

I was visibly shaken by the thought of such a scenario unfolding and thought of how wrong marriage would be for Mark. My head was spinning. Mark doesn't have the ability to even comprehend what marriage is, let alone what the responsibilities of having a wife would be. Is it possible Carla could sink low enough to actually pull something like this off or was Mark being manipulated to say these things to see what kind of reaction I would have? From past experience I think she just might be cruel enough to arrange a marriage. Bringing a wife into the mix would certainly eliminate any chance of me being a part of his life. If he was married to a close acquaintance of Carla's at a legal ceremony his wife would have complete say over his affairs. Overwhelmed, I couldn't stop thinking of Mark's vulnerability and in the wrong hands how easily he could be lead down a very detrimental path.

Immediately, I contacted my lawyer and told him the latest information we'd received from Mark, emphasizing the way he described the ring in great detail. Our lawyer was taken aback by the news. Having met Mark in his office he realized what an injustice would be done if plans were to go ahead and Mark and Dianne were to actually tie the knot. It was apparent by his reaction he was convinced of Carla's lack of morals and felt there was a possibility she would try to get away with something as devious as this but he also warned us there was nothing we could do about the situation until after the marriage occurred. At that point we could try to have the marriage annulled. Wow, what a position to be put in. There seemed to be no end of nasty tricks when it came to Carla but this little scam seemed to reach another all time low.

The New Year came and went and still, no sign of being able to visit with Mark. It infuriated me every time I contacted him by phone. I resented having to go through Carla to speak to my brother. Our conversations were shared with Carla listening in and coaxing Mark on what to say. Most calls were dominated by Carla pressing Mark to insist I had his money and ended with him getting angry with me when I denied his accusations. Time and time again when our conversation was going along smoothly I would hear Carla urging Mark to ask about his money and to find out what I had done with it. She was fully aware of what the outcome would be as she took advantage of Mark's innocence, egging him on until he was so frustrated and angry with me he would hang up. Pitting brother against sister was an antagonistic and cruel game she played. The mere fact she would take advantage of Mark's naivety showed the disregard and lack of respect she had for him and confirmed my labeling her a moral deviate.

My heart went out to Mark, knowing how he was being treated like a puppet. Under normal circumstances I would have never condoned his behavior or the way he spoke to me but knowing how he was being played by Carla I had to make allowances. His incapacity for understanding how he was being manipulated prohibited me from explaining the truth of what was actually going on. Mark's understanding and needs are very primal. In his eyes, he was dependant on Carla for his every need and any disapproval of her was a threat to his very survival. So, it was important to remain indifferent towards her when speaking to him. The crazy thing is if the tables were turned and I was his caregiver, Carla would be in my position. Mark was aware of what side his bread was buttered on and offered his unfaltering loyalty to his caregiver. The reality is, at this point Carla had complete control of Mark, body, mind and soul and it was becoming increasingly difficult to have any kind of relationship with him. Our connection as siblings had deteriorated and I was losing ground with him but for his sake I had to persevere, so I swallowed my pride and shielded my heart against the verbal abuse I was forced to endure during our conversations. I remained indifferent while continuing to make contact with my brother regardless.

The underlying tension between Carla and I was growing with every passing day and if it weren't for the pending court date in September I'm sure I would have waged all out war with her by now. There was still eight months to go before we would know the final verdict. Carla's underhanded move of receiving power of attorney for Mark had put a real ringer into my case leaving me with the job of having her power of attorney reversed by back tracking. Back tracking meant more legality's and more legality's meant more money and unfortunately money was becoming scarce. By now I was weary of the fight but I knew it was necessary to go ahead with whatever the lawyer suggested if I was to ever have any chance of reversing the power of attorney and gaining guardianship of Mark.

From past experiences with the authorities, in regards to gaining access to my brother, I've been forced to accept that being Mark's blood sister as opposed to being his unrelated caregiver is of no consequence in the eyes of the law and I shudder to think of how the importance and integrity of the family unit has crumbled to such a sorry state.

As it turns out, I am now put in the position of having to stifle my anger towards Carla and keep my composure to remain civil while constructing my emails to her, as well as, put up with her insidious intrusions into the private phone calls between Mark and me. You know, there was a time, right after Sarah's death, I was considering allowing Carla to care for Mark as long as I held guardianship of him and had the final say in his care. Now, when I think of the possibility of Carla caring for him I can't believe

I was actually considering that as an option and I have to ask myself, *what on earth was I thinking?* Of course, at that time I was under extreme duress. My mind, clouded with the grief of my sister's death left me feeling overwhelmed and incapable of thinking straight. However, since that time there have been so many red flags warning me of the dangers of allowing Mark to remain with her. At this point I couldn't even imagine her caring for him and my only hope was that a judge would look at both sides and be able to see her devious behavior through my eyes.

The dead of winter and its treacherous road conditions made long distance travel impossible. Therefore, any thoughts of planning a visit with Mark were put on hold and contact with Mark was limited to occasional phone calls. Carla's obvious influence over Mark became quite evident in the disrespectful, short tempered manner he spoke to me. I also sensed by the sound of his now listless voice that his spirit had been broken. He still had no input on anything and continued to ask Carla's opinion about the slightest thing. It broke my heart to hear him fumble with his thoughts only to depend on Carla to complete them for him. Strangely, that only reinforced why I continued to make sure I had regular contact with him. I had to keep faith in believing that justice would be served and Mark would finally be returned to his family.

I continually reminded Carla of my existence through emails to let her know, whether she liked it or not, I was still lurking on the sidelines. Every message

I sent I continued to ask if she would allow us to take Mark off her property for a family get together and each time she reminded me that Mark would not be leaving the property until after the court hearing. It was heart breaking to have to wait until then to be able to see Mark but there was no alternative. Carla had complete and utter control of the situation and she was quite aware of it.

March was around the corner and I sent a message to Carla asking if we could take Mark out to dinner for his birthday. Expecting the same rejection as our previous requests you can imagine my surprise when she agreed to allow us to pick him up so we could celebrate his birthday and spend some time with him. I found it hard to believe she finally agreed to allow us to take him out. I was so excited at the prospect of seeing Mark I began calling everyone in the family to invite them to help us celebrate with him, so plans were made for everyone to meet for a night of fun with Mark being the star attraction. One of Mark's all time favorite things to do was to take part in karaoke. His excitement shone through when I called to tell him we'd planned a karaoke night out for his birthday.

Our day began early to make it in time to pick Mark up and our anticipation grew with every mile. He was all set to go when we arrived at Carla's and after a short drive we arrived at our destination. As Mark entered through the doors of the karaoke bar he was bombarded with a crowd of well wishers, nieces, nephews, aunts, uncles and cousins, leaving Mark overwhelmed and overjoyed. It didn't take long for the party to get into full swing as everyone became comfortable with getting up on stage. Grouped in the most unlikely combinations they all did their best at singing their hearts out. It was such fun and Mark was very happy, but sadly our time together came to an end. On the ride back home Mark rambled on nonstop about how much fun he'd had and had us promise to do it again soon!

As much as we would have loved to spend more time with Mark, Carla had other plans. I don't know what caused her to go back to insisting he not be taken off her property but the next time I emailed her requesting another visit with him she was quite clear about letting us know Mark would not be leaving the property with us until after the court hearing in September and was clear that any visits would be done in her home under her supervision. My guess is Mark had just a little too much fun with us for her liking.

September was six months away which at that time seemed like an eternity. I couldn't wait for everything to be settled once and for all. Of course, I was hoping the judge would somehow see the injustice in abducting someone's brother from them and keeping him hostage. It seemed to be a no brainer to me but I knew it all boiled down to the judge's attitude towards vulnerable people. When I took that into account I wasn't so sure of things going in my favor. I only had to think back to my involvement with the detective and the prosecuting attorney after Mark was abducted from us to bring me back to the reality that things could go either way.

I just couldn't see putting myself in the position of having a visit with Mark in Carla's house with her sitting right there in the room, so I accepted the fact, for the time being, my contact with Mark would be strictly by phone and contact with Carla would be done through email. I continued to bombard her with requests to allow us to take Mark out for the day resulting in the same answer of, "No, not until after court in September." Unbelievably, one day she agreed for us to see Mark at his trailer for a few hours in August. I was stunned and couldn't believe she was allowing us to meet with him alone. Mind you his trailer was behind her house at the far corner of her property but as long as she kept her distance and gave us some private time alone with him it didn't matter.

I saw this window of opportunity as a chance to hold another reunion, so I began calling everyone in the family to invite them to Mark's for the day. When the day finally arrived and vehicle after vehicle full of familiar faces began to show up Mark stood there in amazement and was soon assured he was the feature attraction. We even got to meet Dianne as she drove up in her car and boldly infused herself into the crowd. Making sure everyone was aware of her presence. She then, without notice, sauntered into Carla's house never to be seen again. Ergo, proof positive Dianne was not mentally handicapped and most likely not Mark's fiancé at all but just another cruel figment of Carla's imagination carried out to antagonize us. Mark was in his glory as everyone made a fuss over him but at the end of the day the party was over and it was time to say goodbye. I found the sadness I felt when we waved goodbye reminiscent of when we were kids and had to leave him behind at Cumberland.

When we arrived home there was an email from Carla waiting for me. She said Mark was left overwhelmed, confused and upset because we brought all those strangers to see him that day and asked us not to do that again. More to the truth Carla was the only stranger that day, she was not familiar with Mark's extended family and had no idea who Mark's relatives were, so I just smiled to myself and deleted her message.

As court was fast approaching and we made ourselves busy with finalizing our plans for Mark's care, we were confident we had come up with a very appealing plan. The house we purchased for Mark and Kerrie to live in was close to being completely renovated and Kerrie was preparing to move to Fairport to step in as his caregiver. Also, we were close by to keep an eye on things and help with his care if needed. In addition, we'd met with the association in our area and they were available to us for times when we needed extra help with Mark's care. Also, there was a Friendship Group in town Mark could join that was specifically geared for those with mental disabilities. Most importantly, Mark would be with his family, people who knew his special needs and loved him. We felt confident that our plan was doable and hoped a judge would see it as the best alternative.

The will stated Sarah's estate was to be divided equally between Carla, Mark and me but it had been over eighteen months since Sarah's death and we hadn't heard anything from Carla regarding the settlement of Sarah's house and belongings. Accordingly, a letter was sent out to force Carla to produce a statement for the settlement of assets. With exerted effort we received a complete account of the estate from Carla's lawyer.

The financial statements were almost laughable and fully fulfilled Doug's prophecy that Carla would make sure Mark or I would never reap the portion of Sarah's estate that was due to us. After carefully looking over the figures we saw Carla had falsified the financial documents by showing extravagant amounts of money paid out for maintenance of Sarah's tiny house and property, as well as, exceptionally high records of what it cost to maintain the property. She took the same approach with Mark's maintenance. She had everything backed up with receipts but looking closer I recognized some familiar names. Carla knew full well the more she could claim as expenses the less money would appear to be left in the estate.

Looking over the paperwork regarding the estate I noticed Carla had taken Robert to court to obtain the house. She claimed, as executor of the estate she was entitled to continue with the pending court case on Sarah's behalf. After taking a closer look I realized at the time of purchase, the house had somehow been put into Carla's name and there was nothing to indentify it as ever being part of Sarah's estate. The house was transferred from Robert to Carla for two dollars plus a cash settlement of ten thousand dollars in order to make Robert go away. "Unbelievable!" I mumbled under my breath as I recalled Robert's claim, "It's worth it for me to be done with Carla and just walk away." It was quite clear that sadly I wasn't the only one being shafted.

By the looks of the papers we were presented with, Carla had succeeded in making everything look as if there was very little equity left in the estate. Of course she had receipts to back everything up but it was obvious she'd inflated all expenses and deflated all assets with a lot of help from her friends submitting fraudulent invoices and receipts. The business was no exception. Puppies that Sarah sold for fifteen hundred dollars Carla claimed were sold for sixty dollars. Sarah had fourteen puppies running around the kennel the day she was killed. Not to mention the six world class studs and bitches left behind that were sold for two hundred when Sarah would receive upwards of ten thousand dollars apiece. She claimed the contents of the kennel sold for peanuts.

When we were at Sarah's place two days after her death I remember her computer sitting beside the front door. I thought about taking it with me but for whatever reason I didn't. This oversight gave Carla a window into mine and Sarah's lives, allowing her to distort and make claims that, taken out of context, were misleading. Regretful, but in my defense, I had no idea what was in store for us.

Shockingly, the financial statement showed that twenty-five thousand dollars of Mark's trust fund was deposited into a joint savings account Matt and Sarah had apparently opened up together. The deposit took place only days before my sister's death. Then, immediately after Sarah was killed the entire deposit of twenty-five thousand dollars was moved over in fifteen hundred dollar increments into Carla's personal bank account within a span of three weeks. There was no mention of the forty-five thousand dollars but my guess is it somehow went to benefit Carla.

The deceit was clear after going through page after page of distorted figures but to contest what she was claiming would mean having a thorough forensic audit done to prove any wrongdoing on her part. As much as I would have loved to order an audit I realized it would cost an excessive amount of time and money to have it completed and where I stood with my own finances I simply couldn't afford to have one done. My main concern right then, was gaining access to Mark, so taking a loss on my portion of the estate was something I had to accept if I intended to focus and follow through with reversing the power of attorney and gain access to my brother. This would mean that Mark would go without his fair share of the estate also. Regardless, I was forced to concede and accept the financial records Carla so smugly produced.

The statement she prepared for the judge consisted of nearly two hundred false and misleading claims about Doug and me. To read through the statement she prepared you would have thought she was a close friend who knew everything about me. She even claimed that she was the one who spent caring for my mom during her final days and that mom had asked her personally to take care of Mark. How dare her! She was nowhere near my mom at the last. She was willing to say anything that would make her look closer to the family than she actually was.

At sometime during the pending court case I was asked by Carla's lawyer if I realized Mark had a problem with choking. I had never known Mark to choke and after telling the lawyer that he somehow managed to turn my answer around, as proof that I was not as close to Mark as I was claiming, because if I was close to him I'd know he chokes. His accusation left me blindsided. This twisted inference left me feeling disturbed at how easily things can be turned around. This was not the first time I'd heard of Mark choking. Carla told the police officer about Mark having a problem with choking the night she spoke to Mark in the sunroom. The officer claimed he thought Carla was possibly setting up an alibi by planting the seed that Mark chokes. Hearing this again caused me to seriously consider she might actually be setting up an alibi for herself. I suddenly felt prey and no match against Carla's evil ways.

Not surprising, Carla also included in her statement an album containing a few pictures of Mark with her and her family and a dozen letters from her friends promoting Carla as an upstanding citizen and the best person to have Mark under her care. Keep in mind, these letters exalted Carla to sainthood and pointed to me as a lowlife. Strangely, I didn't know any of the people who submitted their recommendation of Carla and they didn't know me. This led me to wonder if these Carla worshipers actually existed or were they a mere figment of her imagination that she herself had created on paper.

While thumbing through the picture album I stopped when I came across a photo of Cumberland Regional Centre. The building was very impressive, a vast brick facility lumbering over some thirty odd tiny white cottages, dotting the well maintained grounds leading down to Lake Nipissing. Another photo showed the interior of one of the cottages. A handwritten inscription was boldly printed in red ink across the top and read, 'Mark's Childhood Home'. My heart sank as I took in the large one room barrack. Sterile and inhumane came to mind as I looked at the fifteen rows of white cots, all made up with tattered white linen, lining either side of the room. The dingy white walls were peeling and covered with smudges of grime and just to add to the ambiance there were two massive, thickly painted metal doors flanking either end that were kept secured by two massive, rusting locks.

That picture said a thousand words and held a lifetime of pent up emotion concerning my brother. Yes, I am ashamed to say, this was my brother's childhood home. I had stood in that room a number of times as a child and even though I wasn't responsible for placing Mark in Cumberland I was still left with a deep seated feeling of shame. That captioned picture was so powerful it brought me to my knees. After carefully mulling over the contents of the album, Doug and I wondered if we should put together an album of our own in our defense. After all, I had a whole trunk full of family pictures to choose from and I'm sure we could have mustered up a few people who would vouch for our character. When we suggested this to our lawyer he told us not to bother wasting our time. He was sure the judge wouldn't even give it a glance.

"Judges have better things to do than to waste their valuable time looking through picture albums." He stated.

It was easy to see but very hard to swallow the fact that Carla had achieved what we knew she intended to do right from the start. She managed to do Mark and me out of our fair share of the estate. I could understand her wanting to get her hands on my share but what about Mark's share? Carla could easily pull the wool over his eyes without him even knowing it and he would have no idea of what was going on. He was so vulnerable and far be it for me to try to tell him what Carla was doing after her convincing him it was me who took all his money. There was no way of getting around her schemes, so I placated myself by looking forward to the day when Mark was safe under my roof and I could just wash my hands of her.

Then, as a last minute attempt to discredit me I received a request from Carla's lawyer to have a mental capacity test done because Carla didn't feel I had the where with all to have Mark left in my care.

How ridiculous! I was so humiliated going to the doctor to be tested. My mother always said, "You can't un ring a bell". Once you say something you can't take it back and Carla knew this only too well. She knew by sending this request she would be casting doubt on my ability to function as Mark's guardian. She stopped at nothing to cast doubt on my ability to gain guardianship of Mark.

Our case was slated for September 12. With less than a week to go news came over the television that the suit filed by the residents of Cumberland against the government for two billion dollars had been settled. Apparently, if the government was willing to issue a public apology to the residents they would take a financial settlement of thirty-five million dollars. This would mean a difference of having a few thousand dollars being doled out to each resident as opposed to hundreds of thousands of dollars as originally thought. I felt torn with mixed emotions. On one hand I was sorry they settled for so little but on the other hand because Carla held power of attorney over Mark. I was secretly happy to hear the lesser amount was settled upon because in the end I was convinced Carla would never allow Mark to receive any benefit from his settlement.

~ Chapter Fourteen ~

*"It's hard to turn the page when you
know someone won't be in the next chapter
but the story must go on."
~ Thomas Wilder*

In the early morning hours of September 8, 2013, Doug and I were startled by the phone ringing. It was the lawyer calling to say the judge wanted to hold a private meeting with Carla and me for ten o'clock at the courthouse. We weren't given any details and having no idea of what was in store for us we were left feeling cautious and hesitant knowing something out of the norm was in the works. Given such late notice we had to hustle to make it to the meeting on time. When we arrived our lawyer greeted us and ushered us into a council room to wait for the proceedings to begin. While we waited our lawyer explained that it was very unconventional for the judge to request to speak to the both of us privately. Rattled by this change of protocol the lawyer put us on guard to expect just about anything. At that moment I felt very vulnerable, insecure and frightened of what lay ahead. Suddenly, I didn't feel so confident.

After what seemed like an eternity Carla and I were led into the courtroom. We were placed at opposite ends of the table from each other with our lawyers seated beside us. Everyone stood as the judge entered the room and took his place on the other side of the table. Immediately the lawyers began their legal banter and when he finished the room fell silent. Eventually, the judge broke into the silence by going into a lengthy rant about Carla and me agreeing to disagree, letting bygones be bygones, in other words kiss and make up for Mark's sake. We both nodded our heads in agreement but we both knew there had been too much water under the bridge and that was not about to happen, at least not any time soon. As I sat there feeling like a child sitting in the principal's office being chastised for some schoolyard disagreement, I was in disbelief. Had this judge not read any of the material I submitted to him about Carla's unusual conduct and illegal behavior? I suddenly felt my first inklings of defeat in the pit of my stomach.

The judge continued by saying he'd read all the paperwork handed to him and commented on how impressed he was with all the photos and letters submitted by Carla. "Oh my God!" I blurted out, desperately trying to stifle my reaction. I just couldn't believe what I was hearing. It was difficult for me to wrap my brain around the fact a well-versed judge could be impressed by a few photos and a handful of contrived letters. Immediately he proceeded to dismiss all guardianship applications, as well as, our request to have the power of attorney reversed, saying definitively. "None of this will be necessary now!" I sat stunned. Just like that, all we had so wholeheartedly fought for was for naught and it became clear to me where this case was heading.

Without skipping a beat the judge looked straight at me and stated, "Regardless of how this power of attorney was obtained by Carla, I'm telling you there isn't a judge who would overrule it in a court of law and one day both of you will thank me for saving you a lot of time, money and effort fighting for something that will never happen. **"Therefore, Mark will remain under Carla's care and you will be allotted visitation privileges."** His words echoed in my ears as my world crumbled around me.

Suddenly, I found myself caught up in a whirlwind of signing papers. Because of winter weather conditions Doug and I were given access to Mark on the first weekend of every month from March until November including a mutually agreed upon one day visit just before Christmas, again, depending on road conditions. Carla was ordered to install a private land line telephone, to be paid for out of Mark's trust, so Mark and I could communicate with each other freely. The next condition was that Carla was to keep me posted of any medical or legal procedure regarding Mark. When he stated we were both responsible for our own legal costs I heard a rather loud gasp come out of Carla and as I looked over I saw her jaw drop in disbelief. It was obvious she was counting on us covering her costs. With that the proceedings were over but not before the judge told both Carla and me if we had any differences we were to contact a mediator to try and work things out and warned us. "If either of you show up in this courtroom again you'll wish you hadn't!"

Humiliated, defeated and in complete disbelief of the unbelievably bizarre nightmare that had just unfolded in that courtroom, I made my way home to try to make sense of it all. How could they have taken Mark from his family who loves him and hand him over to someone who has done nothing but betray his confidence, take advantage of him and only uses him for her own selfish needs? I was so sure the truth would prevail. I went back over every detail but as much as I tried to sort through the muck and the mire of Carla's existence in my family's lives I was at a loss to make sense of any of it. The grief I felt for the loss of my brother coupled with the loss of my sister was almost more than I could bear.

The following morning I was contacted by the association to tell me they would like to assign Carla to begin authorizing any funding funneled through them and would like to send me the forms to sign so they could transfer the authorization over to her.

"What! What are you telling me?" I exclaimed.

"Well you know Robin, she does have power of attorney over Mark and he will be remaining with her."

"But she was only given power of attorney over his personal affairs not his finances!" I quickly pointed out.

"I'm sorry Robin. It'll just be simpler this way. We will be sending you the forms to sign. We hope you understand." They responded.

I jumped in. "You've got to be kidding! You know as well as I do this will only serve to allow Carla free reign over his funding. You saw for yourself how she tried to push through fraudulent receipts and you know all the deceit she carried out with Sarah's estate. I can't believe you're doing this knowing full well how devious she is and all you can say is it's just easier this way! If you want to give her signing authority to sign for his funding go ahead but don't expect me to sign it over to her." I hung up, retreating to my room shaken and in disbelief at how everyone seemed to take the easy way out; the cops, DA's office, the lawyer, the judge and now the association. It was as though they all shied away from getting involved with Carla opposed to seeing justice served. I guess it was just easier that way.

I don't know how many days I remained locked in the solitude of my own mind but at some point I came to the realization I had no choice but to embrace the judges' ruling and all the injustices I'd witnessed if I wanted to somehow get on with my life. My spirit was broken while I wondered how I could have been so disillusioned with the authorities and the justice system to think they would see through Carla's façade or place any significance on the infinite bond between siblings.

After years of putting up with Carla's disruptive existence in our lives we were eager to meet with her face to face in a court of law. In fact, we were looking forward to having the truth laid out before the court. Holding back from showing Carla our true feelings all these years, so as not to appear to be bitter or scorned was a near impossible feat but somehow we remained poised through it all. Figuring our real reward would be in knowing her true colors would finally be put on display for all to see we remained steadfast. Instead, it all vanished when a shallow minded judge made a trivial decision void of sufficient consideration of the facts. Obviously, a judge who was blindsided by Carla's charming photo album and her deceptive letters leading him to believe this case to be frivolous; a mere schoolgirl spat. Because of this we were denied our 'day in court' after being so sure of Mark finally coming home.

It was very difficult for us to accept our newly appointed relationship with Mark based on the court ordered guidelines the judge set out. However, Carla also had court appointed guidelines to follow in order for Mark to have some sort of structured contact with Doug and me. We mutually agreed to meet halfway to exchange Mark when it was our turn to have him for the weekend. I waited patiently for two months to remind Carla of the court order to install a land line for Mark's use. He was still using Carla's cell phone when he called and Carla wasn't shy about prompting him on what to say. After one particular trying phone call with Carla butting in on our conversation I decided it was time to bring her attention to the neglect of following the court order by sending her an email.

In no uncertain terms her reply made it clear she had no intensions of having a phone installed. Now, all of a sudden we were at war over the phone installation; me insisting, her refusing. I became so furious with her insolence I told her that I was going to order a phone to be installed in his room and I would pay for it myself. Arrangements were made with Bell and from what Mark said a week later he had his very own land line installed in his room next to his bed with my number on speed dial. It was little price to pay for Mark and me to be able to speak to each other privately. We were thoroughly enjoying our conversations without Carla's interruptions for a few days until one day I called Mark and was taken back when I heard the ungodly, irritating screech of a fax machine.

I was left no choice but to send her an email asking if she could unhook Mark's phone from the fax machine. She replied that she couldn't do that because she had a lot of faxing to do in regards to him. Absolutely ridiculous! After one month of listening to the annoying sound of the fax machine every time I called and still not being able to make contact with Mark I had the service in his room disconnected. I should have known Carla couldn't leave well enough alone. If there was any way of getting under my skin she would find a way, even if it meant going against a court order. The only resource I had to settle this disagreement was to hire a mediator but after paying all our legal fees, paying someone to help settle our spats was out of the question, so I was forced to accept things on Carla's terms and she knew it.

Within a few short months Mark would become very angry with me when he came for his visits. He told me Carla said he didn't have to listen to me because I wasn't the boss of him and he'd obsess over the money he was told I stole from him. It didn't take long before his behavior would escalate to a point where Doug would have to hold him back from attacking me. I'm afraid to say but I believe Carla embedded so many untruths into Mark that our relationship quickly deteriorated to the point of no return. Carla had effectively alienated my brother from his family and as much as it pains me to say, to this day, Mark remains with Carla, isolated in her home totally dependent upon her for his very existence.

Doug and me were left disillusioned by Mark's fate. Feeling completely helpless we questioned what the future would hold for him? We couldn't even begin to imagine the latitude of Carla's influence on him. Given the court's blessing to have full reign over Mark she would be free to use his innocence and naivety to her own selfish advantage. She'd already proven that she would go to any lengths to get what she wants and if that means using an unsuspecting mentally handicapped man to get her way then that's what she'll do.

Shortly after our so called 'day in court' I received a call from Marjorie Wilson, the designated capacity officer from Fairport who came to our home to assess

Mark just before Christmas 2011. She sounded very upset. Apparently she'd received a call from Carla telling her she'd better change her assessment findings of Mark being incapable of handling his affairs because Mark had appointed her power of attorney and now after the court hearing nothing on the assessments meant anything. Marjorie felt threatened and wanted to know what to do. This made little sense to me and not knowing what to say I suggested she call my lawyer and ask him what to do about Carla. Marjorie was a very sweet older woman and I felt sorry for her getting tangled up in this mess. I know how frightening Carla could be and I empathized with her.

The thoughts of Carla having court appointed authority to remain in and constantly intrude in our lives left us dreading what the future might hold. Left waiting for the next situation to erupt was, to say the least, unnerving. Doug and me were two broken people in dire need of the sun to shine in our lives once again. We found the purchase of 'Buttercup' our '52 MG gave us a diversion from all the heartache we were feeling. We just couldn't wait for Mark to visit to take him out for a ride. He would be delighted.

'Buttercup' kept us preoccupied with entering into local car shows and parades. Mark happened to be visiting with us a couple of times for the weekend when we showed 'Buttercup in parades. He just loved it. Doug and me took pleasure in taking many day trips. We'd leisurely drive to parts unknown, exchanging waves and glances from everyone we passed. It was great fun! But when all was said and done we were still left with the nagging thoughts of Carla's hold on Mark and her abrasive presence in our lives.

I found it necessary to email Carla to ask if she would mind bringing Mark to our place the next time she was visiting her son in the nearby town of Oakridge because Doug was ill and wasn't able to make the usual halfway exchange. We were surprised when she emailed back that her son had been transferred back to the Port Elgin police station after the court hearing. I suddenly realized how it made perfect sense why we had the feeling we were being harassed by the police while Mark stayed with us after Sarah's death.

One time Doug was pulled over just out of town when helping to move a friend back to the city. The police said they suspected the trailer of being stolen and demanded Doug show the trailer rental slip. He was then asked to completely empty the trailer on the side of the road. Then they drove off leaving Doug to reload the trailer entirely on his own.

When we had Mark staying with us after Carla returned from China we happened to notice an unusual amount of police presence whenever we were parked in town. A number of times walking out of a store we'd find a police car parked beside us or parked behind us appearing to be recording our license plate number. We once discovered them parked right in front of us in the parking isle and had to ask them to move so we could get out. I can now see now how obvious it was that they were keeping track of us. We began to feel like criminals but didn't know what to do about it. After all, we couldn't call the police!

I was hoping with the trial being over and done with, Carla's senseless nonsense would end. I was hoping to be able to grieve the loss of my brother in peace. But I soon realized Carla had other plans. One morning I answered the phone to a Royal Bank of Canada executive asking me about the discussion I'd had with the teller when I was trying to track down Mark's trust fund. Apparently, Carla had filed a complaint about her. She felt the teller had overstepped her bounds by asking me if the name Matt Turner rang a bell and when I told her it did, he was Sarah's employees' husband she replied "There may be criminal activity here." Carla was insisting she had no right to tell me anything and the poor unsuspecting teller had violated the privacy act. Carla was looking to have her dismissed. For a brief moment after I hung up I almost felt sorry for Carla. How bitter and unhappy she must be to feel she has to lash out at everyone who she thinks has wronged her. It made me sad.

Not long after my encounter with the RBC, Dick Branson called to let me know he just completed a final article, at the insistence of Carla, on the status of Mark's trial decision. During our conversation Dick informed me that he felt compelled to send for Carla's theft transcripts after the article came out in the paper. He now knew the truth about all her lies about blaming Mark for stealing from Wal-mart and said he felt bad about her using Mark as her fall guy. In this latest article Carla was quoted as saying, "The case was not about Mark, I already had Mark. It was about vindicating all the accusations made against me." Then she gloated, "I won!" Again, I had to ask myself, at *what cost Carla, what cost?*

We continued to have our court ordered visits with Mark as scheduled. He still didn't have a court ordered landline, so we were left to depend on Carla's grace to help Mark place a call to us. In 2015, Doug became very ill and we were no longer able to take part in the monthly exchange. Visits to our home came to an immediate halt. I couldn't take the chance of Mark losing his temper with me without Doug being able to restrain him, therefore we had to demote ourselves to phone calls only which were becoming fewer and farther apart as time went on. Left with little means to deal with her deficient sense of duty to keep Mark and me connected leaves me not knowing where to turn to next.

In the spring of 2016, my beloved Doug passed away after a lengthy illness. Since then calls from Mark have all but ceased. I can't tell you the last time I heard from him and as I am left to consider his fate. I wonder w*ill he meet the same demise as my sister? Has Carla established an alibi? Will he choke?* I have no way of knowing for sure but what I do know for sure is Mark remains with her to this day. So, I helplessly wait, fully aware of the injustices I know to be true, not knowing where to turn for help.

Epilogue

Originally, keeping a record of the bizarre and unacceptable conduct Carla exhibited quite early in the development of this experience, was my way of keeping track and understanding the constant confusion playing out in my life. What soon developed was a distinctive timeline showing the senseless cruelty directed towards my family. Being naïve and unable to make sense of what was going on around me my writing became infused with heightened emotions. It wasn't until after I took time to read the makeshift journal I realized I had a compelling story to tell.

Initially, the condensed facts merely spilled onto the paper but as time went on the accumulation of injustices began to jump off the page. Years of being physically and emotionally involved in this exceptional course of events only served to intensify how deplorable the violations were. Armed with the truth and laced with passion the timeline evolved into the writing of this book.

After reviewing the mounds of information available to me I felt justified in claiming my family had been repeatedly victimized, in a decade long encounter, by a predator. The deliberate, self serving lies and actions of this woman have left my entire family feeling vulnerable and violated after witnessing and living through the work of what we felt was pure evil.

From the time our paths crossed I suspected a hint of deceit with any encounters having to do with this predator but I was left with unfounded accusations because of the lack of solid proof. Foreign to anything I'd ever experienced before, I was left doubting myself. Unfortunately, giving her the benefit of a doubt only allowed her the time she needed to fully embed herself into my siblings' lives.

In the grand scheme of things my story is a mere glimpse into some of the injustices our social system allows. Due to the rapidly increasing aging population there will be an influx of scenarios similar to the one my family experienced because they are out there, 'predators', waiting and ready to pounce upon their unsuspecting victims.

As parents of the severely handicapped grow older and pass away, their unprotected sons and daughters are in danger of being left under the care of a narcissistic predator. Similarly, as society in general ages and reaches a point in their lives where they are forced to enlist a caregiver, the door is left wide open for a predator to step in and take over any and all of their inheritances and life altering decisions.

As time went on the obvious injustices emitted from all areas of the justice system became perfectly clear. I was left to believe our laws in regards to appointing power of attorney and our laws surrounding being appointed executer of a will need to be readdressed. Predators tend to gravitate to the most vulnerable. Their charm is undeniable. The skill in which they integrate themselves into self-serving situations is incredible. Their web of deception is all but impervious. With an ever growing Senior and disadvantaged population we must somehow find a way to protect the ones who are not capable of protecting themselves. I feel a sense of urgency here.

I can't tell you how many times I've asked myself if I'd done enough to protect my sister or my brother from harm. Could I have been smarter, stronger or more aggressive in fighting for their sakes? I honestly don't know what more I could have done under the circumstances but for whatever reason I feel responsible for the decay of our family. I ask myself *what if it was my own children who were in need of my protection. Would I be able to come through for them?* I'd have to say no, not a chance if I was pitted against a demented soul who was masterful in deception and skilled in twisting the truth.

I don't believe this plot was entirely premeditated by the predator right from the start, rather, I do believe it was more a case of an evolving scenario. Carla, being a skilled opportunist, took advantage of each situation, twisting and turning every opportunity to her advantage regardless of the carnage left in her wake. Simply put, this entire scenario was merely a prime example of the right circumstances coming into the hands of the wrong person. I do believe this predator was involved in some way with my sister's death and am left wondering if my brother will meet his demise at the hands of Carla when he becomes worth more to her dead than alive.

There are some who will come away from reading this book viewing it as a general interest story. Others will experience my book and applaud the intensity of the plot. Then, there are those who will tap into the passion behind my writing but in reality this is a true life experience that me and my family were forced, through no fault of our own, to endure.

Considering each and every one of us will find ourselves in a vulnerable state at some point in our lives I should think the information contained between the pages of this book would be of interest to most readers. These predators are out there waiting for the perfect time to pounce. Readdressing the existing laws affecting the vulnerable in our society with compassion and empathy needs to become a priority with the powers that be.

Clearly, throughout this timeline of events there are many unanswered questions that continue to haunt me to this day. I'm sure you have probably experienced times, when you were reading through the pages of this book, where you had to stop and ask yourself, *how was that possible?* Or you were compelled to take a moment to scratch your head and wonder, *how could that happen?* I am almost certain they would be the same events I am left struggling with.

The bare facts have been laid out as they happened. If what I have reflected on these pages moves you to express your opinion, I would like to hear from you. I would be interested in hearing your suggestions and knowing your thoughts and opinions.

Bewildered, confused and left with no recourse I remain in a state of hopelessness. In my heart of hearts I would like to see this predator brought to justice. Second to that, my hope is to bring to light the primitive and out dated laws, still in existence, to help protect the vulnerable.

Just imagine if the laws pertaining to the appointment of "power of attorney" and "executor" were readdressed. What if, societies most vulnerable, those who cannot speak for themselves, would be given the support and protection needed to guard them from the many opportunists and predators lurking in the shadows? Keep in mind, any one of us could find ourselves vulnerable at some point in our lives. Wouldn't you rest a little easier knowing your final wishes or the wishes of your loved ones would be carried out as intended in a fair and just manner?

Robin Stone

Thank you for reading my story. If you have any questions or suggestions or would like to share your own experience please contact me at robinstangledweb@gmail.com

CPSIA information can be obtained
at www.ICGtesting.com
Printed in the USA
LVHW092315090221
678844LV00003BA/50